YEADON'S REGISTER

of

L N E R

LOCOMOTIVES

Volume Twenty- Eight

**Class R1, S1, T1 &
the WM&CQ Eight-coupled tank**

i

YEADON'S REGISTER OF L.N.E.R. LOCOMOTIVES - VOLUME 28

EDITOR'S NOTE & ACKNOWLEDGEMENTS

The standard number of pages used in each volume of *Yeadon's Register* can be considered as ninety-six but this has been expanded on occasion to group together a number of classes which have some kind of commonality, theme or similarity. This volume, in order to keep within those guidelines, has actually gone in the opposite direction and contracted to eighty printed pages. However, this is just a one-off and Volume 29 will revert back to a somewhat larger size in the number of pages.

This volume of the *Register* covers the pre-Group eight-coupled tank engines inherited by the LNER from three of the constituent companies - the Great Central, Great Northern, and the North Eastern. Volume 28 also marks the completion of the coverage of the eight-coupled locomotives owned at one time or another by the LNER.

Unlike some of the classes recently featured in *Yeadon's Register*, none of the locomotives found within the pages of this volume were preserved - perhaps their less than glamorous lifestyle and, in the main, isolated places of work kept them out of the public eye.

Eric Fry's patience with the editor continues unabated even through 'lean' periods when material for proofing virtually ceases to arrive and then suddenly turns into an avalanche. Unperturbed by any amount of numbers, Eric's dedication and enthusiasm never cease to amaze.

Thanks to Mike and Tina for doing a superb job in the typesetting department. Thanks also to Amadeus Press in keeping up the quality of printing with which we seem to have taken for granted but in fact is appreciated as each volume is published.

Jean and Simon, although thousands of miles away, continue to support the series and give their full blessing - thanks.

The next *Yeadon's Register of LNER Locomotives*, Volume 29, contains the repair history of the popular Great Central Railway 4-4-0 tender engines.

The Yeadon Collection is available for inspection and anyone who wishes to inspect it should contact:-
The Archivist
Brynmor Jones Library
University of Hull
Hull
HU6 7RX
Tel: 01482-465265
A catalogue of the Yeadon collection is available.

First published in the United Kingdom by
BOOK LAW PUBLICATIONS 2003 in association with CHALLENGER
382 Carlton Hill, Nottingham, NG4 1JA.
Printed and bound by The Amadeus Press, Cleckheaton, West Yorkshire.

INTRODUCTION

R1

Due to its increasing suburban passenger traffic in the London area at the turn-of-the-century, the Great Northern Railway required a more powerful locomotive than the four-coupled types then struggling to keep pace. A 2-6-2T or 0-6-2T design would probably have given the required power/adhesion ratio but H.A.Ivatt went one better and produced in 1903 an 0-8-2 tank engine which for the period was a locomotive of somewhat massive proportions.

Only one engine, No.116, was at first built which in the event was somewhat fortuitous because the locomotive was rather too heavy for the lines on which it was intended to work.

When first turned out from Doncaster in June 1903, the engine weighed seventy-nine tons of which sixty-six tons was available for adhesion. The 4ft 8in. boiler was the same as those used on Ivatt's 0-8-0 goods engine (LNER Q1, see also Vol.20). The side tanks were long enough to hold nearly 2,000 gallons of water between them. The resultant design gave a maximum axle load of 17 tons. In August the engine was returned to Doncaster for a serious paring of excess weight having been effectively banned from working over the Widened Lines of the Metropolitan Railway. Wasting little time, the engineers tackled the weight problem firstly by swapping the 4ft 8in. boiler for a new 4ft 2in. boiler which was in stock and was in fact one of six such boilers ordered as replacements in 1901 for the Stirling single-wheeler's. Because of the shorter firebox casing on the Stirling boiler, the cab had to be lengthened to take up the difference; at the front end similar allowances had to be made for the shorter boiler barrel and the smokebox was made bigger to accommodate. Further weight reduction was achieved shortening the length of the side tanks by 5ft 4∫in. so that the water capacity dropped to 1,500 gallons. To keep the massive appearance of the original engine, the same boiler cladding was used on the smaller boiler but it was bulked-out to give the illusion. All this was completed in the period from 15th to 25th August 1903. On its return to traffic, No.116 was subjected to trials which proved its capabilities in speeding up the existing schedules.

No further engines of the class, now designated L1 by the GNR (R1 by the LNER), were built until the following year when ten similarly 'doctored' 0-8-2 tanks, numbered 117 to 126, were turned out from Doncaster during the last months of 1904. Like No.116, these ten were equipped with condensing gear for working the Widened Lines and all eleven engines resided at King's Cross shed for Inner Suburban and Metropolitan Line passenger train duties. However their bulk was in some ways their undoing, at least on the Widened Lines, and in 1907, with the introduction of Ivatt's successful 0-6-2T (LNER N1, see also Vol.25), the 0-8-2 tanks were banished from the London area. Although certain members of the class were to return there at various periods, the condensing apparatus, which was superfluous outside the Met. lines, was removed from all eleven engines.

The next batch of R1's came out from Doncaster in the winter of 1905. These ten, Nos.127 to 136, were intended largely for goods work in Nottinghamshire and the West Riding where weight restrictions were not so stringent although some colliery branches barred their 15 ton plus axle load. The smaller boiler was used throughout.

The final, and largest, batch of Class R1 came out from Doncaster during the latter half of 1906. Numbered 137 to 156,

they too had the 4ft 2in. boiler even though they were all intended for and indeed did work from Colwick, Ardsley and Bradford. Strangely, all had the low boiler mountings and cab roof which had been a necessary part of the design to permit use on the Widened Lines.

The 4ft 2in. diameter boiler hurriedly fitted to No.116 in August 1903 was as mentioned earlier one of six already in stock. During the period 1904-06 another forty of these boilers were constructed for the R1's. These though had two-ring instead of three-ring barrels and no spares were made. One more of the type used on No.116 was used by No.128 from 1910 to 1921. A further odd boiler was carried by No.117 from 1911 to 1920. This had been made in 1900 and came from 2-2-2 No.872, and had a two-ring barrel with a taller dome set further back.

Incidentally, after rebuilding of the class with 4ft 8in. boilers began in 1909, gaining pace during 1912-13, the relatively young 4ft 2in. boilers found further use on Gresley's new J51 class 0-6-0T's introduced in 1913, which were designed with this in mind. The barrel had to be shortened and thirty-seven were so used, including the three odd boilers referred to above.

The 4ft 2in. diameter boiler, with its smaller firebox, meant that the engines were rather 'under-boilered'. Once the class had left the London area there was no real need to keep down their weight, so in July 1909 No.133 was fitted with a 4ft 8in. boiler of the original pattern. In fact there were still nine of these unused boilers left over from the original order before the 4ft 2in. type was substituted. During 1912-13 twenty-three more of the class were similarly rebuilt - four of these were fitted with the unused boilers, the remainder received second-hand boilers as recorded below. The rate of rebuilding slowed thereafter and it was not until No.3154 was dealt with in August 1926 that the task was complted.

Because the length of the firebox was 8ft 0in. on the 4ft 8in. boiler, whereas it was only 6ft 2in. on the 4ft 2in. type, a shorter cab had to be fitted. The opportunity was taken to increase its height (except in the case of Nos.117 and 128, rebuilt in 1921) and taller boiler mountings were employed. The first rebuild, No.133, also kept a low cab at first, but had been brought into line later.

The larger boilers were standard with those used on the Class Q1 and Q2 0-8-0 engines. During 1912-15 thirty new boilers with superheaters were ordered for fitting to the 0-8-0 engines, releasing their saturated boilers for re-use on Class R1. From 1919 other second-hand boilers of this type came from Class C2 Atlantics. The earliest boilers on this class had a deeper firebox and were therefore unsuitable for use on the eight-coupled engines, the shallow firebox type later being adopted as standard for all the classes concerned.

Finally, five new boilers were made in 1929, the only saturated boilers to LNER Diagram 4 to be constructed since 1909. Incidentally, the 4ft 8in. boiler with which No.116 had been built was not wasted and saw further service on Class C2. It eventually found its way back to Class R1, being used on No.3145 from December 1922 to its December 1927 withdrawal.

Seven R1's received superheated boilers, the first being No.136 in June 1914. This boiler had a Robinson pattern superheater and came from a Q1. No.131 was the next, in July 1916, and got the twin tube type, also from a Q1. Two new Robinson superheated boilers were fitted to Nos.129 and 149 in June 1917, and two more Nos.135 and 138 were superheated in

(above) One engine, No.116, was built in June 1903 at Doncaster with 4ft 8in. diameter boiler and long side tanks holding 2000 gallons of water. This was Ivatt's attempt to cure the adhesion problems with the four-coupled tanks then used for London suburban trains on the Metropolitan widened lines to Moorgate. However, the design proved too heavy for the Metropolitan City widened lines on which it was to work goods trains. Doncaster works. *(below)* The other side of No.116 in Doncaster works yard before being finish painted and showing what could have been regarding mobile billboards. In the few weeks when it worked briefly into and out of King's Cross in June - August 1903, its long tanks carried this advertising and it was alone in having the company name spelt in full. By August 15th 1903 No.116 was back at Doncaster works for rebuilding, which was immediately expedited and took no more than ten days to complete.

Four engines, Nos.1170 to 1173 were built during December 1907 and January 1908 by Beyer, Peacock and Co. Manchester, for hump shunting duties on the Great Central.

May 1918. Their new boilers were equipped with Schmidt superheaters, spare from Class C1 engines. The final conversion was No.148 in May 1920 which got a second-hand boiler with Robinson superheater off a Q1.

All seven engines remained superheated, the Robinson type eventually becoming standard. Nos.129, 131 and 136 did not previously carry 4ft 8in. saturated boilers - the others did.

The 19∫in. diameter cylinders would have been ideal for use with a 4ft 8in. boiler but the smaller boiler necessary for the weight reduction meant that the engines were 'over-cylindered'. This was recognised at first by placing 18in. inserts inside No.120's cylinders in June 1905. No.116 got the same treatment in the following November; the other nine were re-cylindered during 1906-07, all to 18in. diameter. The redundant cylinders were re-used on Class Q1 0-8-0's then being constructed at Doncaster. Nos.127 to 136 came out in 1905 with 19∫in. cylinders, butthe final twenty engines had 18in. cylinders. In general the smaller cylinders were bored out to 19in. when the bigger boiler was fitted whereas the 19∫in. (later quoted as 20in.) were retained.

At the outbreak of WW1 all the class had settled at Colwick shed, the last seven of the original ten working in the West Riding having left the area in early 1914. Colwick used the engines mainly on coal trains with occasional use on local passenger working. Besides the colliery trips bringing coal to Colwick yards and returning empties, certain of the superheated engines worked coal trains from Colwick as far as New England, bringing back empties for the Nottinghamshire and Derbyshire pits.

In 1919 six R1's were sent to King's Cross for empty passenger stock workings from the terminus out to Hornsey carriage sidings. These six were replaced during 1920 and 1921 by another six from Colwick, all newly painted in GNR green livery. These latter half dozen R1's stayed in the Capital until 1929 when four of their number returned to Colwick and two, Nos.3137 and 3156 moved out to Hornsey for shunting duties in the carriage sidings there; this was the pair's last employment before their withdrawal in July 1931.

Withdrawal of the class had begun in December 1927 with the class pioneer No.3116 along with 3127, 3145, 3153 and 3155 going for scrap. The final member of Class R1 No.3154, was condemned in February 1934.

S1

In December 1907 two locomotives emerged from Beyer, Peacock's works in Gorton and made the short trip across the Great Central main line into the precincts of the locomotive works opposite. These engines were the first of four massive 0-8-4 tank engines, numbered 1170 to 1173, being built for the Great Central Railway by the Manchester company. The next two arrived at the GC works a month later.

Intended to work the new hump yard at Wath, these three-cylinder giants tipped the scales at 99 tons with nearly 76 tons available for adhesion.

Designed by J.G.Robinson, the GCR Class 8H tanks (LNER Class S1) were based on Robinson's 0-8-0 tender engines (LNER Class Q4) [see also Volume 20] with the same size coupled wheels and axle spacing. The middle cylinder was added to give more evenly distributed power whilst pushing loaded coal trains over the Wath hump. Power reversing gear was fitted for the three sets of Stephenson motion.

The boiler employed on the S1 class was larger in diameter and grate area than those used for the Q4 engines and was similar to the boiler used on the 4-6-0's of GCR Class 8C (LNER B1/

B18) and 8F (LNER B4) [see also Volume 22] also on the Atlantics (LNER C4 and C5) [see also Volume 13].

So that the recently commissioned Whitemoor yard in Cambridgeshire could have the benefit of powerful humping engines, the LNER built two more S1 class engines, Nos.2798 and 2799, in early 1932. Basically the same in outline as the GC engines, one major and several minor detail changes had been made to them. Erected at Gorton and emerging respectively in May and June 1932, these were even heavier than their former GC counterparts, weighing in at 104˜ tons but they were equipped with boosters.

The boosters fitted to these new engines were a pair of three ordered in 1929, unique in the fact that they were reversible. The third set was fitted to No.6171 in January 1932. The booster engine replaced the rear bogie and allowed the full locomotive weight to be used for adhesion during shunting operations. Prior to the idea of fitting a booster, the authorities had resorted to double heading two S1's at Wath when the weather conditions were less than ideal for moving the extremely heavy coal trains over the hump. No.6171, with its booster fitted became the heaviest engine in the class at nearly 104° tons.

The new engines, the booster fitted original engine, and the three unmodified engines created three separate class parts and these were designated S1/3, S1/2 and S1/1 in that order. The boosters were removed in 1943 though they were taken out of use from about 1940. The reversible element was never used on the new engines after experience with No.6171, in the early months of 1932, revealed possible problems with the booster bogie springing when running in reverse. The special modified bogies used to house the booster stayed with the three engines to withdrawal.

The four GC built engines were all fitted with saturated boilers of the type introduced for the Atlantics in 1903. In 1909 a new boiler was built to allow exchange within the class. From 1912 various second-hand boilers from the C4 and C5 classes saw further use on S1 class along with two more new ones. Superheating started for the S1 engines when No.6171 was fitted with a booster in 1932. Its superheated boiler had come from an O4 No.6219 which had used this type of boiler after it was introduced for the that class in 1911 (see also Volume 24A). The supply of saturated Diagram 15 boilers eventually ran out and Nos.6172 and 6173 were superheated in 1940 and 1941 respectively. No.6170, by now numbered 69900, was not superheated until December 1951.

When new in 1932, Nos.2798 and 2799, had superheated boilers very similar to Diagram 15 but these were separately classified Diagram 105. The main difference lay in the crown of the inner firebox which was sloped slightly downwards from front to back in order to minimise the risk of being uncovered by water whilst working over the hump at Wath yard. However, these two boilers (Nos.8464 and 8465) were not confined to these two engines (see tables). Second-hand Diagram 15 boilers were fitted from time to time on Nos.2798 and 2799. Stragely, 2798 (as 69904) finished its days with its original boiler.

Mexborough shed was responsible for the Wath engines in GC days and in fact through all of the LNER period whilst those engines sent to Whitemoor were maintained by March shed.

Wath yard contained two humps and each hump employed two S1's virtually round the clock from midnight Sunday to 6.00 a.m. the following Sunday. During the late afternoon each day two Q4's took over so that the S1's could return to shed for an hours coaling, watering and any necessary maintenance for which an hour was allowed (for further information on the S1's work

3

Ten engines, Nos.1350 to 1359 of North Eastern Railway Class X, were built at Gateshead between September 1909 and April 1910. Note they did not have plating to the two coal rails, but this had been added before Grouping when they became LNER Class T1.

at Wath *see* Part 9B of the RCTS *Locomotives of the LNER*).

No.6170 went to March for three weeks in April 1930 for trials at the new Whitemoor Up yard after which it returned to Wath. The two new 1932-built engines went to Mexborough for Wath yard duties after release from Gorton and this allowed Nos.6172 and 6173 to move to March in July of that year for working the Whitemoor hump; these two stayed at March until December 1949 when diesel motive power took over their hump work. Whilst at March the S1's worked a similar round-the-clock regime to their counterparts at Wath and their relief when servicing requirements called was usually the ubiquitous O4. From March shed the two S1's, by now numbered 9902 and 9903, went to Frodingham where they were used for shunting duties in the yards. After a year they returned to Mexborough which now became responsible for the whole class.

Having six S1's to do the work of four was something of a luxury but no other work could be found other then humping Wath yard. When BR introduced the 350 h.p. diesel shunter onto the Wath duties the days of the S1 class were numbered and by the end of 1953 they started to drift away from Mexborough. First to go was 69903 which went to Immingham for dock shunting, followed a month later by 69904. The others went to Doncaster where they spent most of the time in store. The Immingham pair did not find permanent employment either; 69903 was condemned in March 1954 and 69904 transferred to Doncaster shed. Nos.69901 and 69905, the latter after a general repair, went to Frodingham in April 1955 for a further spell of yard shunting which they carried out until withdrawn in January 1957, the last of the S1's. The Doncaster engines had been condemned the previous January.

The working life of three of the class had spanned nearly fifty years whilst a fourth member had completed forty-seven years service which by any standard is not a bad innings especially for the specialist work involved.

T1

The need for powerful shunting locomotives to move the huge

amount of coal being mined in this country prior to the Great War became ever more acute shortly after the turn of the century. As mentioned above the GCR tackled the problem at the newly built marshalling yard at Wath by building four large eight-coupled tank engines to push the vast quantities of Yorkshire mined coal over the hump there. The North Eastern Railway had their problem multiplied by having large yards at four locations all in the business of receiving and sorting full and empty coal wagons, two in Yorkshire and two in County Durham. So, in September 1909 Wilson Wordsell introduced his 3-cylinder Class X 4-8-0 tank locomotive (LNER Class T1). Built at Gateshead works, a total of ten T1's had emerged by April 1910 to satisfy the needs of the Traffic Department.

Numbered 1350 to 1359, these engines weighed-in at just over 84° tons in working order with nearly 67 tons available for adhesion. The saturated boiler was smaller than the GC engines at 4ft 9in. but it was basically the same boiler as was carried by the NER 4-6-0 passenger tank engines.

In November and December 1925, another five T1 engines, numbered 1656 to 1660, were built by the LNER, this time at Darlington works. Except for having Ross 'pop' safety valves instead of the Ramsbottom type, the boilers on the five LNER built engines were identical to the North Eastern built T1's.

Altogether the fifteen class T1 engines carried five types of boiler at one time or another, although all were 4ft 9in. diameter and the same basic size. Only one engine carried a superheater.

Diagram 61: This was the type first fitted to the whole class and was the same as that introduced two years earlier on the Wordsell A6 class engines. Down to 1930, fifteen replacement boilers of this type were constructed for use on both classes. The last one was taken out of service in August 1957 when No.69916 (1357) was withdrawn. This engine, and the two withdrawn in 1937, were the only T1's that carried only Diagram 61 boilers throughout their lives.

Diagram 63B (saturated): By 1945 the need had arisen to replace the Diagram 61 boilers that first served the 1925 built T1's. The 63B type had by then been adopted as standard for use on the A6, A7 and A8 classes (*see* also Volume 21). A superheater was fitted but this equipment was thought to be unnecessary for the work undertaken by Class T1 (although due to a misunderstanding at Darlington works one engine had already been given a superheated 63B boiler - *see* below). During 1945 five 63B boilers without superheaters were constructed specially for use on Class T1. Five more followed during 1950-52, of which four went to Class T1 and one to an A7. Previously the superheater had been removed from a 1939-built 63B boiler and this went to No.69915 (1356) in October 1949.

The 63B type had a barrel rolled from a single plate and visibly differed from the earlier designs in having the dome set 1ft 9in. further back, the cover being of squarer, less rounded shape. Except for the three T1 engines which always had Diagram 61 boilers, all the others received the 63B saturated type and ended their lives with them, except for Nos.69917 and 69919 which changed later to earlier variants.

Diagram 63A: Had been introduced in 1929 for use on the Class H1 4-4-4 tanks, all subsequently rebuilt to A8. One of these boilers had its Robinson superheater taken out in July 1955 and then spent its final years on 69917 (1359) until engine and boiler were withdrawn in November 1959.

Diagram 63B (superheated): The final version of the 63 type introduced in 1939 it was intended for use on Classes A6, A7 and A8. As already mentioned, in September 1944 No.1354 (later 69914) needed a new boiler and was given a superheated one in error. This singularity survived a boiler change to another 63B superheated boiler in August 1949. The engine reverted to saturated in December 1951, when a Diagram 63B saturated boiler was provided.

Diagram 63C: This had been the first redesign of the 63A type to make it fully interchangeable among Classes A6, A7 and A8. Only five of these boilers were made, in 1935. One of them was later converted from superheated to saturated and fitted to No.69922 (1660) in December 1949. In September 1952 this boiler passed to No.69919 (1657) which retained it to withdrawal in February 1955.

Individual use of the various Diagram 63 boilers on Class T1 will be found in the tables.

The original Wordsell engines went to work at Gascoigne Wood, Hessle Yard (Hull), Newport and Tyne Dock and, except for No.1359's move to Gateshead in 1924, stayed on those same duties until the late 1920's when economic conditions altered traffic flows. The 1925 engines were set to work at Hull (1), Newport (1) and two new venues for the class, Stockton (2) and York (1). Nos.1358 and 1656 went to March in January 1929 to hump shunt the about to be opened Up yard at Whitemoor. Another T1, No.1355 of Tyne Dock was exchanged with No.1656 in June 1932 and the two T1's spent another couple of years at March before moving to Doncaster in April 1934. These two never returned from the Southern Area with both spending time at Mexborough shed and further stints at Doncaster still looking for suitable employment. No.1355 went to King's Cross as shed shunter in 1936 but stayed there for less than two months before returning to Doncaster. With economic conditions against them the two T1's entered Doncaster works in May 1937 and were scrapped, their boilers being sent to Stratford as stationery steam plant where they worked until March 1945.

The closure of Stockton yard in 1930 brought further re-allocations of the class during that year. New territory was trod when Nos.1658 and 1660 transferred to the former Hull & Barnsley Railway shed at Bullcroft and spent nearly a year there on the Warmsworth pilot duty before going to Dairycoates. The latter shed had five of the class by the end of 1939 all employed locally but by 1952 they had all left Hull and were concentrated

at just three sheds: Newport (8), Stockton (3) and Tyne Dock (2).

During the 1950's the class was again on the move, Selby, York, Consett and even the former Lancashire & Yorkshire shed at Goole having them allocated. The latter shed got Nos.69918 and 69921 in 1957 for work at the docks there, marshalling coal wagons amongst other goods.

Withdrawals started again in 1955 when 69914 and 69919 were condemned. The following year saw just 69922 withdrawn whilst in 1957 three of the class were scrapped. Just one went in 1958 but 1959 nearly finished the class when five were condemned that year leaving just one survivor No.69921 which hung on at Tyne Dock until June 1961.

WM&CQ 0-8-0ST

Becoming eventually No.400B in the Great Central Railway Duplicate List, this 0-8-0 saddle tank locomotive had certainly had an interesting life. Acquired when the GCR absorbed the Wrexham, Mold & Connah's Quay Railway in 1905, this engine was built as an 0-6-0 tender engine for the Manchester & Birmingham Railway in 1846 by Sharp, Stewart & Co. It later became the property of the London & North Western Railway who rebuilt it to saddle tank form in 1858.

In January 1872 it was put on the LNWR Duplicate List and later that year it was purchased by the WM&CQ. This latter company rebuilt the engine too, giving it a new boiler and another set of driving wheels in 1880 to produce a rigid wheelbase 0-8-0ST. In 1888 after eight years of employment on the Buckley branch where its long wheelbase was totally unsuited, it was again rebuilt, this time to an 0-6-2ST.

Two years later it was involved in an accident at Connah's Quay and for the next two years it went through another rebuilding process whereby it acquired new frames with a new tank atop the 1880 boiler. Still an 0-6-2ST, No.6 as the Wrexham company had numbered it, the engine was rebuilt yet again in 1903, reverting to its 0-8-0ST guise and acquiring a new boiler. In this condition it was handed over to the GCR, probably with nothing remaining of the original 1846 engine.

All its work was done in the Wrexham area but responsibility for its maintenance passed to Gorton works which carried out at least one general repair in 1915.

The GCR numbered the engine 400 in 1905 and between then and 1912 it was put on the GC Duplicate List and became 400B, its last number before scrapping.

When the LNER came into being this engine was unique in being the only 0-8-0ST that the company inherited but its LNER career was short lived because in August 1923 the engine was condemned and cut up at Gorton before it could be allotted either an LNER number or class.

On 25th August 1903 No.116 was out with its weight reduced from 79 to 70¼ tons and the maximum axle load was reduced from 17 to 15¼ tons. The tanks were shortened by 5ft 9¾in. which cut the water capacity to 1500 gallons. The boiler diameter was now 4ft 2in. instead of 4ft 8in. but this was not apparent as the clothing plates were not adjusted but the cab was lengthened to suit. As altered, No.116 proved acceptable, so a production batch could go ahead. Doncaster shed.

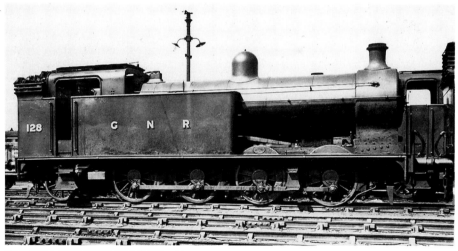

From August to November 1904 Nos.117 to 126 were built at Doncaster. These were followed during October to December 1905 by Nos.127 to 136, and from May to October 1906 by Nos.137 to 156 which completed the class. As new, Nos.117 to 126 were similar to No.116 as altered but, the condensing apparatus was removed from these eleven between July and October 1907. Nos.127 to 156 never had that apparatus. Length of cab, and position of dome show that a 4ft 2in. diameter boiler was fitted.

Transfer away from the London District enabled reversion to the 4ft 8in. boiler to be made. This started in July 1909 with No.133 and by Grouping only Nos.130 and 154 still had 4ft 2in. boiler. No.128 was rebuilt in June 1921.

CLASS R 1

3116

Doncaster 1004.

To traffic 7/1903.

REPAIRS:
Don. ?/?—?/8/03.**G.**
4ft 2in. dia. boiler fitted.
Don. ?/?—?/9/13.**G.** *Rebuilt.*
Don. 14/6—11/10/19.**G.**
Don. 11/4—28/7/23.**G.**
Don. 12/10/25—9/1/26.**G.**

BOILERS:
1536.
1388 *(new)* ?/8/03.
1409 *(exQ1 3416)* ?/9/13.
6966 *(exQ1 3447)* 11/10/19.

SHEDS:
King's Cross.
Colwick ?/07.
King's Cross ?/19.
Colwick ?/20.

RENUMBERED:
3116 9/1/26.

CONDEMNED: 30/12/27.
Cut up at Doncaster.

———————————

3117

Doncaster 1056.

To traffic 8/1904.

REPAIRS:
Don. ?/?—?/10/11.**G.**
Don. 20/10/20—16/4/21.**G.**
*Rebuilt & carriage heating
apparatus fitted.*
Don. 23/2—9/5/25.**G.**
Don. 11/6—9/8/28.**G.**
Don. 7—28/2/31.**G.**

BOILERS:
1615.
  872 *(exSingle 872)* ?/10/11.
1539 *(3127)* 16/4/21.
7344 *(3147)* 28/2/31.

SHEDS:
King's Cross.
Colwick ?/07.

King's Cross 4/21.
Colwick 14/2/29.

RENUMBERED:
3117 9/5/25.

CONDEMNED: 20/4/33.
Cut up at Doncaster.

———————————

3118

Doncaster 1057.

To traffic 8/1904.

REPAIRS:
Don. ?/?—?/2/13.**G.** *Rebuilt.*
Don. 7/4—3/7/20.**G.**
Don. 22/8—15/12/23.**G.**
Don. 7/4—17/7/26.**G.**

BOILERS:
1614.
1543 *(exQ1 3425)* ?/2/13.
6965 *(ex3134)* 15/12/23.

SHEDS:
King's Cross.
Colwick ?/07.
King's Cross ?/19.
Colwick ?/20.

RENUMBERED:
  118N 15/12/23.
3118 17/7/26.

CONDEMNED: 18/1/29.
Cut up at Doncaster.

———————————

3119

Doncaster 1058.

To traffic 8/1904.

REPAIRS:
Don. ?/?—?/9/13.**G.** *Rebuilt.*
Don. ?/?—?/5/16.**G.**
Don. ?/?—?/11/18.**G.**
Don. 25/2—19/8/22.**G.**
Don. 15/1—11/4/25.**G.**
Don. 3/3—6/7/28.**G.**

BOILERS:
1613.

1571 *(exQ1 3444)* ?/9/13.
1574 *(exQ1 3408)* ?/5/16.
1566 *(ex3138)* ?/11/18.
1541 *(ex3123)* 19/8/22.

SHEDS:
King's Cross.
Colwick ?/07.
King's Cross ?/19.
Colwick ?/20.

RENUMBERED:
3119 11/4/25.

CONDEMNED: 16/10/30.
Cut up at Doncaster.

———————————

3120

Doncaster 1059.

To traffic 8/1904.

REPAIRS:
Don. ?/?—?/10/13.**G.** *Rebuilt.*
Don. ?/?—?/6/19.**G.**
Don. 31/10/22—24/2/23.**G.**
Don. 24/4—11/7/25.**G.**

BOILERS:
1616.
6967 *(exQ1 3448)* ?/10/13.
1574 *(ex3119)* ?/6/19.

SHEDS:
King's Cross.
Colwick ?/07.

RENUMBERED:
3120 11/7/25.

CONDEMNED: 11/7/28.
Cut up at Doncaster.

———————————

3121

Doncaster 1060.

To traffic 8/1904.

REPAIRS:
Don. ?/?—?/4/14.**G.**
Don. ?/?—?/4/19.**G.** *Rebuilt.*
Don. 4/10/21—28/1/22.**G.**
Don. 28/11/23—2/3/24.**G.**

Don. 26/7—27/11/26.**G.**
Don. 11/5—29/6/29.**G.**

BOILERS:
1618.
6767 *(ex3136)* ?/4/14.
1483 *(exC2 3255)* ?/4/19.
1401 *(ex3122)* 2/3/24.

SHEDS:
King's Cross.
Colwick ?/07.

RENUMBERED:
3121 2/3/24.

CONDEMNED: 14/9/31.
Cut up at Doncaster.

———————————

3122

Doncaster 1061.

To traffic 9/1904.

REPAIRS:
Don. ?/?—?/10/11.**G.**
Don. ?/?—?/1/14.**G.** *Rebuilt.*
Don. 10/10/19—24/1/20.**G.**
Don. 6/3—22/9/23.**G.**
Don. 4/1—27/3/26.**G.**
Don. 2/2—2/3/29.**G.**
Don. 11/4—9/5/31.**G.**

BOILERS:
1622.
6766 *(ex3135)* ?/10/11.
1401 *(exQ1 3430)* ?/1/14.
1554 *(ex3124)* 22/9/23.
1410 *(exQ1 3427)* 27/3/26.
8229 *(new)* 2/3/29.

SHEDS:
King's Cross.
Colwick ?/07.

RENUMBERED:
  122N 22/9/23.
3122 27/3/26.

CONDEMNED: 2/12/33.
Cut up at Doncaster.

———————————

WORKS CODES:- Bpk - Beyer, Peacock. Cow - Cowlairs. Dar- Darlington. Don - Doncaster. Ghd - Gateshead. Gor - Gorton. Inv - Inverurie. Str - Stratford.
REPAIR CODES:- **C/H** - Casual Heavy. **C/L** - Casual Light. **G** - General. **H**- Heavy. **H/I** - Heavy Intermediate. **L** - Light. **L/I** - Light Intermediate. **N/C** - Non-Classified.

(above) **No.130 had a 4ft 8in. boiler when ex works 29th September 1923, but on No.154, out on 8th March 1924 as No.3154, the 4ft 2in. boiler was retained until it next went in for repair in April 1926. Out on 7th August 1926 it had been dealt with, only 16 months prior to the first withdrawals of the class.**

(left) **The 4ft 8in. boiler was the same as was used by the 0-8-0 tender engines, and as with that class, some got superheaters. Between April 1914 and May 1920, seven, Nos.129, 131, 135, 136, 138, 148 and 149 had a superheater put in. Only on the first two dealt with, Nos.136 and 131, were tail rods put on and a 9in. frame extension was needed to cater for them. Nos.129, 136, 148, 149 had the 18-element type Robinson superheater.**

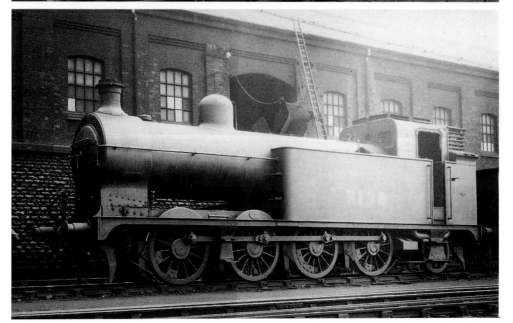

When Nos.135 and 138 were superheated in May 1918, their boilers got second-hand 18-element Schmidt type superheaters taken from large Atlantic's Nos.1452 and 1460. These they kept until 1928 when both changed to Robinson type. Note neither tail rods nor frame extension fitted. Colwick shed.

From July 1916 to April 1927, No.131 was fitted with 17-element twin-tube superheater which accounts for its 4ft 9in. diameter instead of 3ft 11³/₄ in. smokebox door, and the handrails being cut back to end on the side of the smokebox and not curving round on to the front.

At LNER take-over the two engines with 4ft 2in. boiler had cabs 8ft 11¹¹/₁₆in. long but only 12ft 4 ⁷/₈in. high from rail level as first designed to suit the Metropolitan load gauge.

3123

Doncaster 1062.

To traffic 9/1904.

REPAIRS:
Don. ?/?—?/12/13.**G**. *Rebuilt.*
Don. 11/11/21—11/2/22.**G**.
Don. 14/11/23—15/3/24.**G**.
Don. 16/3—17/7/26.**G**.

BOILERS:
1620.
1541 *(exQ1 3429)* ?/12/13.
1407 *(ex3125)* 11/2/22.

SHEDS:
King's Cross.
Colwick ?/07.

RENUMBERED:
3123 15/3/24.

CONDEMNED: 13/9/28.
Cut up at Doncaster.

3124

Doncaster 1063.

To traffic 10/1904.

REPAIRS:
Don. ?/?—?/5/13.**G**. *Rebuilt.*
Don. 1/7—1/11/19.**G**.
Don. 21/2—2/6/23.**G**.
Don. 23/11/25—27/2/26.**G**.
Don. 23/3—27/4/29.**G**.
Don. 11/4—9/5/31.**G**.

BOILERS:
1617.
1554 *(exQ1 3440)* ?/5/13.
1404 *(exC2 3949)* 2/6/23.
7350 *(ex3154)* 27/4/29.

SHEDS:
King's Cross.
Colwick ?/07.

RENUMBERED:
3124 27/2/26.

CONDEMNED: 8/9/33.
Cut up at Doncaster.

3125

Doncaster 1064.

To traffic 10/1904.

REPAIRS:
Don. ?/?—?/5/13.**G**.
Don. ?/?—?/4/15.**G**. *Rebuilt.*
Don. 26/4—30/10/20.**G**.
Carriage heating app. fitted.
Don. 22/3—7/7/23.**G**.
Don. 16/11—31/12/25.**G**.
Don. 9/2—23/3/29.**G**.
Don. 28/2—28/3/31.**G**.

BOILERS:
1619.
6760 *(ex3135)* ?/5/13.
1407 *(exQ1 3426)* ?/4/15.
6967 *(ex3120)* 30/10/20.
8231 *(new)* 23/3/29.

SHEDS:
King's Cross.
Colwick ?/07.
King's Cross 10/20.
Colwick 22/3/29.

RENUMBERED:
3125 2/3/25.

CONDEMNED: 26/8/33.
Cut up at Doncaster.

3126

Doncaster 1065.

To traffic 11/1904.

REPAIRS:
Don. ?/?—?/10/12.**G**. *Rebuilt.*
Don. 15/11/22—17/3/23.**G**.
Don. 25/9/25—8/1/26.**G**.

BOILERS:
1621.
1395 *(exQ1 3406)* ?/10/12.
1411 *(exQ1 3447)* 8/1/26.

SHEDS:
King's Cross.
Colwick ?/07.

RENUMBERED:
3126 8/1/26.

CONDEMNED: 10/1/29.
Cut up at Doncaster.

3127

Doncaster 1097.

To traffic 10/1905.

REPAIRS:
Don. ?/?—?/7/11.**G**

Don. ?/?—?/7/17.**G**. *Rebuilt.*
Don. 7/1—13/3/20.**G**.
Don. 11/7—6/10/23.**G**.
Don. 18/1—10/4/26.**G**.

BOILERS:
6758.
6759 *(ex3128)* ?/7/11.
1539 *(ex3149)* ?/7/17.
1565 *(ex3133)* 13/3/20.

SHEDS:
Ardsley.
Colwick 1/14.

RENUMBERED:
127ɴ 6/10/23.
3127 10/4/26.

CONDEMNED: 30/12/27.
Cut up at Doncaster.

3128

Doncaster 1098.

To traffic 10/1905.

REPAIRS:
Don. ?/?—?/11/10.**G**.
Don. 23/3—18/6/21.**G**. *Rebuilt.*
Don. 8/10/24—17/1/25.**G**.
Don. 16/7—12/11/27.**G**.

BOILERS:
6759.
1391 *(new)* ?/11/10.
1564 *(ex3148)* 18/6/21.

SHEDS:
Ardsley.
Colwick 1/14.

RENUMBERED:
3128 17/1/25.

CONDEMNED: 8/6/29.
Cut up at Doncaster.

3129

Doncaster 1099.

To traffic 11/1905.

REPAIRS:
Don. ?/?—?/7/14.**G**.
Don. ?/?—16/6/17.**G**.
Rebuilt with superheated boiler.
Don. 20/9/22—20/1/23.**G**.
*Hulburd Valveless Lubrication
fitted.*
Don. 8/5—25/7/25.**G**.

Don. 27/9—24/10/28.**G**.
Don. 21/3—25/4/31.**G**.

BOILERS:
6760.
6764 *(ex3133)* ?/?/10.
7344 *(new)* 16/6/17.
1402 *(exQ1 3424)* 25/7/25.
7346 *(ex3138)* 24/10/28.

SHEDS:
Ardsley.
Colwick 1/14.

RENUMBERED:
3129 25/7/25.

CONDEMNED: 10/8/33.
Cut up at Doncaster.

3130

Doncaster 1100.

To traffic 11/1905.

REPAIRS:
Don. 9/3—12/6/20.**G**.
Don. 16/5—29/9/23.**G**. *Rebuilt.*
Don. 1/2—24/4/26.**G**.

BOILERS:
6761.
6759 *(ex spare)* 12/6/20.
1576 *(ex3139)* 29/9/23.

SHEDS:
Bradford.
Colwick 7/13.

RENUMBERED:
130ɴ 29/9/23.
3130 24/4/26.

CONDEMNED: 22/1/29.
Cut up at Doncaster.

3131

Doncaster 1101.

To traffic 12/1905.

REPAIRS:
Don. ?/?—18/7/16.**G**.
Rebuilt with superheated boiler.
Don. 26/10/20—30/4/21.**G**.
Scarab oil firing fitted.
Don. 25/11/21—7/1/22.**G**.
Oil firing removed..
Don. 16/12/23—31/5/24.**G**.
Don. 14/4—8/12/27.**G**.

The two which changed to 4ft 8in. boiler in 1921 got the shorter cab, but were unusual in keeping a low roof. They were Nos.117 (16th April) and 128 (18th June). Between October 1920 and April 1921 the six allocated to empty carriage workings into and out of King's Cross station were fitted with carriage heating apparatus with hose connection at both ends. The pipe between them was on the right hand side, under the running plate. Colwick shed.

When the 4ft 8in. boiler was put on from 1912, a shorter cab was normally fitted but with the height increased by $10^{5}/8$in. Colwick shed.

At LNER take-over, not all had the bunker cage extension usually fitted with the taller cab. In 1920 and 1921 six, Nos.117, 125, 137, 151, 154 and 156 were given green paint and transferred to King's Cross for empty stock workings. Where these had been fitted with a cage, it was taken off. The other 1921 rebuild, No.128, kept the low roof so did not get a cage *(see* page 6, bottom*).*

When the last one got a 4ft 8in. boiler, No. 3154 out on 7th August 1926, no cage was fitted because it was still a King's Cross station shunter.

3131 cont./
BOILERS:
6762.
1549 *(exQ1 3437)* 18/7/16.
8049 *(new)* 8/12/27.

SHEDS:
Bradford.
Colwick 3/14.

RENUMBERED:
3131 31/5/24.

CONDEMNED: 8/1/30.
Cut up at Doncaster.

3132

Doncaster 1102.

To traffic 11/1905.

REPAIRS:
Don. ?/?—?/3/16.**G.**
Don. 30/8/22—13/1/23.**G.**
Rebuilt.
Don. 4/8—24/10/25.**G.**

BOILERS:
6763.
6762 *(ex3131)* ?/3/16.
1566 *(ex3119)* 13/1/23.

SHEDS:
Colwick.
King's Cross ?/19.
Colwick ?/20.

RENUMBERED:
3132 24/10/25.

CONDEMNED: 4/9/28.
Cut up at Doncaster.

3133

Doncaster 1103.

To traffic 11/1905.

REPAIRS:
Don. ?/?—?/7/09.**G.** *Rebuilt.*
Don. ?/?—?/9/19.**G.**
Don. 12/12/22—24/3/23.**G.**
Don. 22/6—27/8/25.**G.**

BOILERS:
6764.
1565 *(new)* ?/7/09.
1558 *(exC2 3984)* ?/9/19.

SHEDS:
Colwick.

King's Cross ?/19.
Colwick ?/20.

RENUMBERED:
3133 27/8/25.

CONDEMNED: 11/7/28.
Cut up at Doncaster.

3134

Doncaster 1104.

To traffic 11/1905.

REPAIRS:
Don. ?/?—?/11/13.**G.** *Rebuilt.*
Don. 12/2—15/5/20.**G.**
Don. 12/2—2/6/23.**G.**
Don. 24/8—21/11/25.**G.**

BOILERS:
6765.
6965 *(exQ1 3446)* ?/11/13.
401 *(ex3146)* 2/6/23.

SHED:
Colwick.
King's Cross ?/19.
Colwick ?/20.

RENUMBERED:
3134 21/11/25.

CONDEMNED: 25/7/28.
Cut up at Doncaster.

3135

Doncaster 1105.

To traffic 12/1905.

REPAIRS:
Don. ?/?—?/9/11.**G.**
Don. ?/?—?/5/13.**G.** *Rebuilt.*
Don. ?/?—25/5/18.**G.**
Superheated boiler fitted.
Don. 1/3—22/5/20.**G.**
Don. 15/8—3/11/23.**G.**
Don. 14/12/25—13/3/26.**G.**
Don. 31/10—7/12/28.**G.**

BOILERS:
6766.
6760 *(ex3129)* ?/9/11.
1573 *(new)* ?/5/13.
7350 *(new)* 25/5/18.
7834 *(new)* 13/3/26.

SHED:
Colwick.

RENUMBERED:
 135ɴ 3/11/23.
3135 13/3/26.

CONDEMNED: 27/9/30.
Cut up at Doncaster.

3136

Doncaster 1106.

To traffic 12/1905.

REPAIRS:
Don. ?/?—19/6/14.**G.**
Rebuilt with superheated boiler.
Don. 19/4—14/10/22.**G.**
Don. 18/5—29/8/25.**G.**
Don. 30/1—28/6/28.**G.**

BOILERS:
6767.
1569 *(exQ1 3445)* 19/6/14.
7137 *(exQ1 3427)* 14/10/22.

SHED:
Colwick.

RENUMBERED:
3136 29/8/25.

CONDEMNED: 9/8/30.
Cut up at Doncaster.

3137

Doncaster 1119.

To traffic 5/1906.

REPAIRS:
Don. ?/?—?/8/12.**G.** *Rebuilt.*
Don. ?/?—?/11/20.**G.**
Don. 6—13/1/21.**L.**
Carriage heating app. fitted.
Don. 8/12/24—20/3/25.**G.**
Don. 1/11/27—21/1/28.**G.**

BOILERS:
6778.
1404 *(exQ1 3412)* ?/8/12.
6968 *(ex3143)* ?/11/20.

SHEDS:
Colwick.
King's Cross 1/21.
Hornsey 22/7/29.

RENUMBERED:
3137 20/3/25.

CONDEMNED: 1/8/31.
Cut up at Doncaster.

3138

Doncaster 1120.

To traffic 5/1906.

REPAIRS:
Don. ?/?—?/5/13.**G.** *Rebuilt.*
Don. ?/?—29/5/18.**G.**
Superheated boiler fitted.
Don. 2/1—14/4/23.**G.**
Don. 15/9—31/12/25.**G.**
Don. 5/3—22/9/28.**G.**
Don. 21/3—18/4/31.**G.**

BOILERS:
6779.
1566 *(new)* ?/5/13.
7346 *(new)* 29/5/18.
8086 *(new)* 22/9/28.

SHED:
Colwick.

RENUMBERED:
3138 31/12/25.

CONDEMNED: 2/12/33.
Cut up at Doncaster.

3139

Doncaster 1121.

To traffic 5/1906.

REPAIRS:
Don. ?/?—?/8/13.**G.** *Rebuilt.*
Don. 14/11/19—28/2/20.**G.**
Don. 21/2—9/6/23.**G.**
Don. 11/11/25—20/2/26.**G.**

BOILERS:
6780.
1576 *(exQ1 3443)* ?/8/13.
1559 *(exC2 3949)* 9/6/23.

SHED:
Colwick.

RENUMBERED:
3139 20/2/26.

CONDEMNED: 8/6/29.
Cut up at Doncaster.

Associated with the taller cab, a cage extension to the bunker was fitted with its top some 2ft 1in. higher than the top of the two coal rails, increasing capacity by half a ton. The sides were splayed outwards at the top, except on No.133 (*see* page 29, top) where they tapered inwards to the top.

During the coal strike of 1921, No.131 (only) was fitted with Scarab apparatus to burn oil fuel. The cage was replaced by a shaped tank which held 900 gallons of oil. It was so fitted when ex works 30th April 1921 but No.131 returned to works on 25th November 1921 for this apparatus to be dismantled. It was out on 7th January 1922 with the normal cage. In the 1926 coal strike, no R1 was fitted for alternative fuel burning.

3140

Doncaster 1122.

To traffic 5/1906.

REPAIRS:
Don. ?/?—?/8/12.**G**. *Rebuilt.*
Don. 25/10/22—24/2/23.**G**.
Don. 19/3—20/6/25.**G**.
Don. 6/12/26—7/5/27.**H**.

BOILERS:
6781.
1406 *(exQ1 3415)* ?/8/12.
1572 *(exQ1 3401)* 7/5/27.

SHED:
Colwick.

RENUMBERED:
3140 20/6/25.

CONDEMNED: 8/1/30.
Cut up at Doncaster.

_____

3141

Doncaster 1123.

To traffic 5/1906.

REPAIRS:
Don. ?/?—?/3/14.**G**.
Don. ?/?—?/5/19.**G**. *Rebuilt.*
Don. 8/5—7/10/22.**G**.
Don. 6/3—21/8/25.**G**.
Don. 5/3—13/6/28.**G**.

BOILERS:
6782.
6781 *(ex3140)* ?/3/14.
1489 *(exC2 3989)* ?/5/19.
1560 *(exQ1 3437)* 21/8/25.

SHED:
Colwick.

RENUMBERED:
3141 21/8/25.

CONDEMNED: 5/6/30.
Cut up at Doncaster.

_____

3142

Doncaster 1124.

To traffic 6/1906.

REPAIRS:
Don. ?/?—?/10/12.**G**. *Rebuilt.*

Don. ?/?—?/6/18.**G**.
Don. 6/2—1/5/20.**G**.
Don. 14/2—6/5/22.**H**.
Don. 3/6—4/10/24.**G**.
Don. 12/5—21/9/27.**G**.

BOILERS:
6783.
1396 *(exQ1 3432)* ?/10/12.
1573 *(ex3135)* ?/6/18.
1552 *(ex3156)* 6/5/22.

SHED:
Colwick.

RENUMBERED:
3142 4/10/24.

CONDEMNED: 10/12/29.
Cut up at Doncaster.

_____

3143

Doncaster 1125.

To traffic 6/1906.

REPAIRS:
Don. ?/?—?/9/13.**G**. *Rebuilt.*
Don. ?/?—?/11/19.**G**.
Don. 29/11/22—24/3/23.**G**.
Don. 14/7—24/10/25.**G**.
Don. 1/2—24/4/26.**H**.
Don. 9/1—14/2/29.**G**.

BOILERS:
6784.
6968 *(exQ1 3449)* ?/9/13.
1548 *(exQ1 3436)* ?/11/19.
8227 *(new)* 14/2/29.

SHED:
Colwick.

RENUMBERED:
3143 24/10/25.

CONDEMNED: 1/8/31.
Cut up at Doncaster.

_____

3144

Doncaster 1126.

To traffic 6/1906.

REPAIRS:
Don. ?/?—?/4/16.**G**. *Rebuilt.*
Don. 5/1—29/4/22.**G**.
Don. 17/7—29/11/24.**G**.
Don. 9/11/25—6/3/26.**H**.
Don. 31/1—26/5/28.**G**.

BOILERS:
6785.
1568 *(ex3155)* ?/4/16.
7344 *(ex3129)* 6/3/26.
1543 *(exQ1 3437)* 26/5/28.

SHED:
Colwick.

RENUMBERED:
3144 29/11/24.

CONDEMNED: 9/8/30.
Cut up at Doncaster.

_____

3145

Doncaster 1127.

To traffic 7/1906.

REPAIRS:
Don. ?/?—?/5/13.**G**. *Rebuilt.*
Don. 20/9—30/12/22.**G**.
Don. 14/4—27/6/25.**G**.

BOILERS:
6786.
1563 *(new)* ?/5/13.
1536 *(exC2 3990)* 30/12/22.

SHED:
Colwick.

RENUMBERED:
3145 27/6/25.

CONDEMNED: 30/12/27.
Cut up at Doncaster.

_____

3146

Doncaster 1128.

To traffic 7/1906.

REPAIRS:
Don. ?/?—?/2/13.**G**. *Rebuilt.*
Don. 5/1—20/5/22.**G**.
Don. 17/2—23/5/25.**G**.

BOILERS:
6787.
401 *(exQ1 3427)* ?/2/13.
1398 *(exQ1 3414)* 20/5/22.

SHED:
Colwick.

RENUMBERED:
3146 23/5/25.

CONDEMNED: 21/2/28.
Cut up at Doncaster.

_____

3147

Doncaster 1129.

To traffic 7/1906.

REPAIRS:
Don. ?/?—?/7/13.**G**. *Rebuilt.*
Don. 23/3—12/6/20.**G**.
Don. 20/6—22/9/23.**G**.
Don. 28/10/25—13/3/26.**G**.
Don. 12/5—12/7/28.**G**.

BOILERS:
6788.
1392 *(exQ1 3402)* ?/7/13.
1563 *(ex3145)* 22/9/23.
7347 *(ex3149)* 13/3/26.
7344 *(ex3144)* 12/7/28.

SHED:
Colwick.

RENUMBERED:
3147 13/3/26.

CONDEMNED: 5/11/30.
Cut up at Doncaster.

_____

3148

Doncaster 1130.

To traffic 7/1906.

REPAIRS:
Don. ?/?—?/10/14.**G**. *Rebuilt.*
Don. 29/1—22/5/20.**G**.
Superheated boiler fitted.
Don. 23/8—1/12/23.**G**.
Don. 4/1—3/4/26.**G**.
Don. 6/4—4/5/29.**G**.

BOILERS:
6789.
1564 *(exQ1 3409)* ?/10/14.
1394 *(exQ1 3411)* 22/5/20.
7650 *(exC2 3983)* 4/5/29.

SHED:
Colwick.

RENUMBERED:
3148 3/4/26.

CONDEMNED: 23/4/32.
Cut up at Doncaster.

_____

Engines which had 18in. diameter cylinders were in GNR Load Class H irrespective of boiler diameter. The indication was given by the cast iron collar on the front stand pipe for the vacuum brake. Colwick shed.

Those fitted with 19¾in. or 20in. diameter cylinders were in Load Class N and carried the appropriate collar.

In the 1924 Southern Area Load Classification, the R1's were rated at 5, but the collars (where carried) all showed 6 on them. No.3156 (*see* page 12, top) continued to carry only N; No.3150 (*see* page 28, top) had both 6 and N.

Along with the fitting of 4ft 8in. boiler from 1909, a built-up chimney 2ft 2$\frac{1}{4}$in. tall was normally put on. Colwick.

At least two, Nos.3119 and 3128, carried a plain chimney which was 2in. shorter than the built-up type. Doncaster shed.

The front ring of the boiler was divided, the two parts being joined by an 8$\frac{1}{4}$in. wide lapping ring. This arose because the tubes were 1ft 8$\frac{5}{8}$in. shorter than the length of the boiler barrel. Doncaster works.

3149

Doncaster 1131.

To traffic 8/1906.

REPAIRS:
Don. ?/?—?/7/13.**G.** *Rebuilt.*
Don. ?/?—23/6/17.**G.**
Superheated boiler fitted.
Don. 1/8/22—20/1/23.**G.**
Don. 1/8—31/10/25.**G.**
Don. 2/2—9/3/29.**G.**

BOILERS:
6790.
1539 *(exQ1 3422)* ?/7/13.
7347 *(new)* 23/6/17.
7198 *(exQ1 3444)* 31/10/25.
8175 *(new)* 9/3/29.

SHED:
Colwick.

RENUMBERED:
3149 31/10/25.

CONDEMNED: 3/7/31.
Cut up at Doncaster.

3150

Doncaster 1132.

To traffic 8/1906.

REPAIRS:
Don. ?/?—?/12/12.**G.** *Rebuilt.*
Don. 28/1—17/4/20.**G.**
Don. 1/2—28/4/23.**G.**
Don. 16/11/25—6/3/26.**G.**
Don. 19/1—2/3/29.**G.**
Don. 2/5—23/5/31.**G.**

BOILERS:
6791.
1538 *(exQ2 3405)* ?/12/12.
1573 *(ex3142)* 28/4/23.
8228 *(new)* 2/3/29.

SHED:
Colwick.

RENUMBERED:
3150 6/3/26.

CONDEMNED: 1/12/33.
Cut up at Doncaster.

3151

Doncaster 1133.

To traffic 8/1906.

REPAIRS:
Don. ?/?—?/5/13.**G.** *Rebuilt.*
Don. 27/10/20—12/3/21.**G.**
Carriage heating app. fitted.
Don. 8/12/24—13/3/25.**G.**
Don. 29/7—14/10/27.**G.**

BOILERS:
6792.
1570 *(new)* ?/5/13.

SHEDS:
Colwick.
King's Cross 3/21.
Colwick 14/2/29.

RENUMBERED:
3151 13/3/25.

CONDEMNED: 8/2/30.
Cut up at Doncaster.

3152

Doncaster 1134.

To traffic 9/1906.

REPAIRS:
Don. ?/?—?/5/17.**G.** *Rebuilt.*
Don. 10/6—28/8/20.**G.**
Don. 19/3—23/8/24.**G.**
Don. 26/7—24/12/26.**G.**
Don. 6/7—3/8/29.**G.**

BOILERS:
6793.
1550 *(exQ1 3438)* ?/5/17.
1561 *(exQ1 3439)* 24/12/26.
8230 *(new)* 3/8/29.

SHEDS:
Ardsley.
Colwick 1/14.

RENUMBERED:
3152 23/8/24.

CONDEMNED: 24/8/31.
Cut up at Doncaster.

3153

Doncaster 1135.

To traffic 9/1906.

REPAIRS:
Don. ?/?—?/2/13.**G.** *Rebuilt.*
Don. 16/8—9/12/22.**G.**
Don. 15/12/24—4/4/25.**G.**

BOILERS:
6794.
1551 *(exQ1 3403)* ?/2/13.

SHEDS:
Ardsley.
Colwick 1/14.

RENUMBERED:
3153 4/4/25.

CONDEMNED: 30/12/27.
Cut up at Doncaster.

3154

Doncaster 1136.

To traffic 9/1906.

REPAIRS:
Don. 28/9—20/11/20.**G.**
Carriage heating app. fitted.
Don. 2/11/23—8/3/24.**G.**
Don. 15/4—7/8/26.**G.** *Rebuilt.*
Don. 5/11—19/12/28.**G.**
Don. 23/5—20/6/31.**G.**

BOILERS:
6795.
7350 *(new)* 7/8/26.
7347 *(ex3147)* 19/12/28.

SHEDS:
Ardsley.
Colwick 1/14.
King's Cross 11/20.
Colwick. 14/2/29.

RENUMBERED:
3154 8/3/24.

CONDEMNED: 3/2/34.
Cut up at Doncaster.

3155

Doncaster 1137.

To traffic 10/1906.

REPAIRS:
Don. ?/?—?/3/13.**G.** *Rebuilt.*
Don. ?/?—?/2/16.**G.**
Don. 1/7—18/11/22.**G.**
Don. 18/3—4/7/25.**G.**

BOILERS:
6796.
1568 *(exQ1 3442)* ?/3/13.
1562 *(exQ1 3428)* ?/2/16.

SHEDS:
Bradford.
Colwick 7/13.

RENUMBERED:
3155 4/7/25.

CONDEMNED: 30/12/27.
Cut up at Doncaster.

3156

Doncaster 1138.

To traffic 10/1906.

REPAIRS:
Don. ?/?—?/3/13.**G.** *Rebuilt.*
Don. 3/8—11/12/20.**G.**
Carriage heating app. fitted.
Don. 20/2—23/5/25.**G.**
Don. 12/1—25/3/28.**G.**

BOILERS:
6797.
1552 *(exQ1 3435)* ?/3/13.
1409 *(ex3116)* 11/12/20.

SHEDS:
Bradford.
Colwick 7/13.
King's Cross 12/20.
Hornsey 22/7/29.

RENUMBERED:
3156 23/5/25.

CONDEMNED: 3/7/31.
Cut up at Doncaster.

WORKS CODES:- Bpk - Beyer, Peacock. Cow - Cowlairs. Dar- Darlington. Don - Doncaster. Ghd - Gateshead. Gor - Gorton. Inv - Inverurie. Str - Stratford. Wrx - Wrexham.
REPAIR CODES:- **C/H** - Casual Heavy. **C/L** - Casual Light. **G** - General. **H**- Heavy. **H/I** - Heavy Intermediate. **L** - Light. **L/I** - Light Intermediate. **N/C** - Non-Classified.

(left) All boilers built before 1927 were fitted with four 3in. diameter Ramsbottom safety valves.

(below) The later boilers were fitted with two 2½in. diameter Ross 'pop' safety valves but only Nos.3122, 3124, 3125, 3131, 3138, 3143, 3149, 3150 and 3152 carried that type. Colwick shed.

When a superheater was put in, lubrication for the cylinders and valves was provided by a Wakefield mechanical type mounted on the leading splasher on the right hand side.

(above) On the seven superheated engines, the vacuum ejector exhaust pipe passed along the outside of the boiler on the right hand side. Colwick shed.

(left) The engines which were not superheated had the vacuum ejector exhaust pipe inside the boiler barrel even on those with 'pop' safety valves. This was a February 1929 built boiler on 3150.

(below) Some of the first ten of the production batch had buffers with taper shank and end collar housing a solid spindle, but only Nos.3117 and 3119 were noted still with this type when in LNER painting. No.121 had taper shank, but as No.3121 the buffers were parallel shank.

By far the most usual type of buffers was the parallel shank with hollow spindle. When new No.116 had that type and by Grouping the only exceptions noted were on 3117 and 3119. Although No.121 moved away in 1907, as 3121 it still carried the twin lamp irons at right hand front corner for codes peculiar to the Great Northern London District. Nottingham (Victoria).

(centre) No.3137 was an oddment by acquiring a smokebox door on which destination board brackets were fitted. The only passenger work the class did in LNER days was the Gedling colliery miners' trains from Nottingham (Victoria) to Daybrook and these had no call for a destination board. In any case No.3137 was a London District passenger shunting engine, and of the six so employed, only this and No.3156 carried the brackets.

(below) Until 1912 all forty-one had GNR fully lined green painting but after the 1914-1918 war only the six allocated to King's Cross passenger shunting, Nos.117, 125, 137, 151, 154 and 156, had the green fully lined livery restored. King's Cross shed.

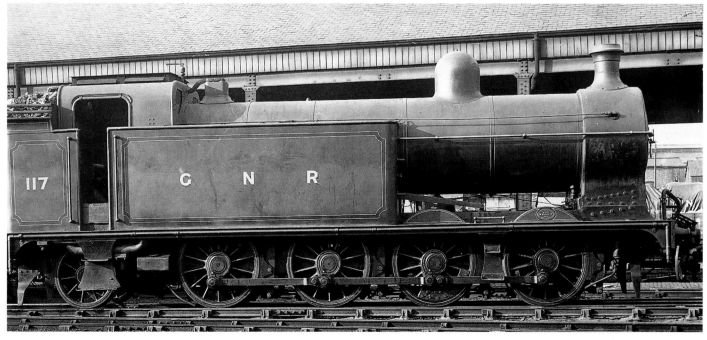

(above) **From September 1912 standard painting was dark grey and without lining and using transfers in white with black shading.**

No.145 was the last one ex works still in GN ownership on 30th December 1922. Although in the normal dark grey with white numbers, its tanks were void of any initials. Colwick shed.

Post-Grouping colour was black and until after June 1928, single red lining was applied. From February to June 1923 the ampersand was included in the company's initials. Note the inward tapering cage on the bunker.

(above) **Ten got this first style: 120 (24th February), 140 (24th February), 126 (17th March), 133 (24th March), 143 (24th March), 138 (14th April), 150 (28th April), 124 (2nd June), 134 (2nd June) and 139 (9th June). The next two done did not have the ampersand: 125 (7th July 1923) and 116 (28th July 1923).**

(centre) **There were seven to which the N suffix was added to the number, all in 1923: 122$_N$ (22nd September), 147$_N$ (22nd September), 130$_N$ (29th September), 127$_N$ (6th October), 135$_N$ (3rd November), 148$_N$ (1st December) and 118$_N$ (15th December).**

The suffix was only put after the number on the tank sides and did not appear on the front buffer beam. Note the 3-link loose coupling.

(above) **Beginning with No.3121, ex works 2nd March 1924, the full LNER number was used and No.3156 shows how the red lining was applied. After the early June 1928 decision to dispense with red lining to reduce the cost of painting, only seventeen of the forty-one had a further repainting at which they got unlined black: 3117, 3119, 3121, 3122, 3124, 3125, 3129, 3135, 3136, 3138, 3143, 3147, 3148, 3149, 3150, 3152 and 3154.**

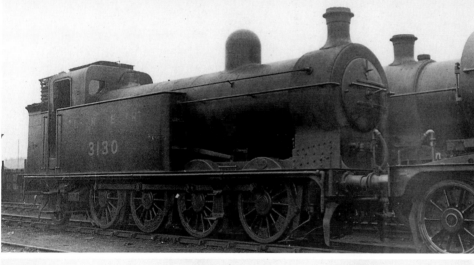

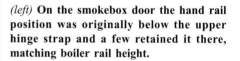

(left) **On the smokebox door the hand rail position was originally below the upper hinge strap and a few retained it there, matching boiler rail height.**

Even before Grouping a start had been made on moving the door rail to a higher position (*see* page 6, bottom) and the majority finished with the rail above the upper strap.

(above) **A rather undignified No.156 at King's Cross shed posing as a 0-8-0 tank, its carrying wheels being out for light repair.**

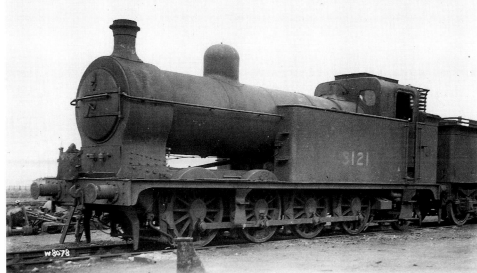

(right) **There was variety in the type of coupling fitted. Many had the screw adjustable whilst others, (see page 27, bottom) made do with the 3-link loose type.**

The cage on the bunker did not unduly prevent access because the base on each side was hinged to open outwards.

There was no uniformity about the position of the works number plate. It was normally on the second splasher but at least eight, Nos.3116, 3119, 3121, 3123, 3126, 3130, 3150 and 3151 had it on the leading splasher. Three, Nos.120, 3137 and 3156 (*see* pages 19, 25 middle and 28, top) did not have works plates at all.

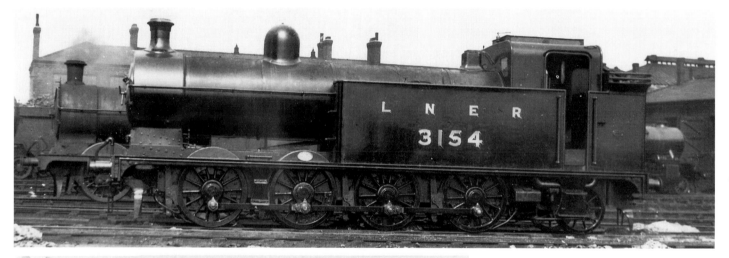

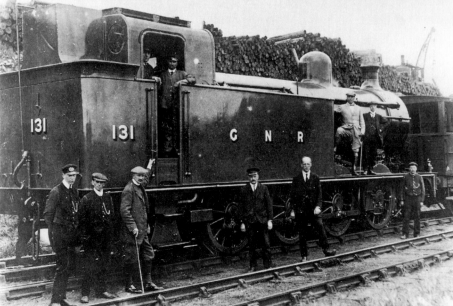

(*above*) After seven went for scrap in 1933 only No.3154 survived and when it too was withdrawn on 3rd February 1934 Class R1 was extinct.

Another view of No.131 when fitted with the Scarab oil fuel firing system. Here, in May 1921, it is, ironically, on trials at Gedling colliery.

No.130 also at Gedling colliery in May 1921 was on typical work from Colwick shed.

One engine, No.6171 was rebuilt on 9th January 1932 with a superheated boiler at Gorton and with a booster fitted bogie which replaced the original bogie.

Two further S1 class engines, Nos.2798 (28th May) and 2799 (25th June), were built by the LNER at Gorton in 1932. They were similar to No.6171 but incorporated several detail alterations. Although externally similar to the Diagram 15 boilers on Nos.6170 to 6173, the new boilers built for 2798 and 2799 had the top of the inner firebox 3³/₈in. lower at the rear than at the tube plate. This was intended to avoid loss of water cover when working on the hump. These two boilers were given Diagram No.105.

CLASS S 1

6170

Beyer, Peacock 5002.

To traffic 12/1907.

REPAIRS:
Gor. ?/?—27/2/09.**G.**
Gor. ?/?—23/11/12.**G.**
Gor. ?/?—31/7/17.**G.**
Gor. 8/4—29/7/22.**G.**
Gor. 9/2—3/5/24.**G.**
Gor. 30/6—25/12/26.**G.**
New centre cylinder.
Gor. 8/6—20/7/29.**G.**
Gor. 12/12/31—23/1/32.**G.**
Gor. 16/2—30/3/35.**G.**
Gor. 30/1—27/2/37.**G.**
Gor. 18/11—16/12/39.**G.**
Gor. 7/10—21/11/42.**G.**
Gor. 6—27/5/44.**L.**
Gor. 30/3—27/4/46.**G.**
New centre cylinder.
Gor. 5/3—2/4/49.**G.**
Gor. 29/9—17/11/51.**G.**
Superheated boiler fitted.

BOILERS:
1331.
  498 *(new)* 27/2/09.
1146 *(exC4 6089)* 23/11/12
1332 *(ex spare)* 31/7/17.
1702 *(exC4 5263)* 3/5/24.
1821 *(exC4 6088)* 25/12/26.
1827 *(new)* 20/7/29.
1702 *(ex6171)* 23/1/32.
1805 *(ex6173)* 30/3/35.
1078 *(ex spare)* 27/2/37.
1807 *(ex6173)* 21/11/42.
1078 *(ex spare)* 27/4/46.
1807 *(ex spare)* 2/4/49.
22222 17/11/51.

SHEDS:
Mexborough.
March 3/4/30.
Mexborough 25/4/30.
Darnall 6/12/53.
Mexborough 13/12/53.
Doncaster 10/1/54.

RENUMBERED:
6170 3/5/24.
9900 28/7/46.
69900 2/4/49.

CONDEMNED: 6/1/56.
*Into Gor. for cut up 18/2/56
but sent to Darlington for
scrapping.*

6171

Beyer, Peacock 5003.

To traffic 12/1907.

REPAIRS:
Gor. ?/?—4/6/10.**G.**
Gor. ?/?—20/6/14.**G.**
Gor. ?/?—25/10/19.**G.**
Gor. 8/1—19/2/21.**G.**
Gor. 6/10—8/12/23.**G.**
Gor. 25/12/26—5/3/27.**G.**
Gor. 8/6—20/7/29.**G.**
Gor. 17/10/31—9/1/32.**G.**
*Rebuilt to Part 2, superheated
boiler & booster fitted.*
Gor. 19/1—23/2/35.**G.**
Gor. 19/3—7/5/38.**G.**
Gor. 4/1—8/3/41.**G.**
Gor. 28/11/42—2/1/43.**L.**
Booster removed.
Gor. 4/3—3/6/44.**G.**
Three new cylinders.
Gor. 6—20/9/47.**L.**
Side rods fractured.
Gor. 4/9—9/10/48.**G.**
Gor. 14/10—11/11/50.**C/H.**
Gor. 31/3—16/6/51.**C/L.**
Gor. 11/4—9/5/53.**G.**

BOILERS:
1333.
1331 *(ex1172)* 4/6/10.
1333 *(exC4 6086)* 20/6/14.
1807 *(new)* 25/10/19.
1702 *(ex6170)* 5/3/27.
  812 *(exO4 6219)* 9/1/32.
8465 *(ex2799)* 7/5/38.
3323 *(exO4 3823)* 9/10/48.
3323 reno.22120 11/11/50.
22188 9/5/53.

SHEDS:
Mexborough.
Doncaster 10/1/54.
Frodingham 10/4/55.

RENUMBERED:
1171c 8/12/23.
6171 5/3/27.
9901 26/5/46.
69901 9/10/48.

CONDEMNED: 1/1/57.
Into Dar. for cut up 5/1/57.

6172

Beyer, Peacock 5004.

To traffic 1/1908.

REPAIRS:
Gor. ?/?—27/3/09.**G.**
Gor. ?/?—19/3/10.**G.**
Gor. ?/?—28/6/13.**G.**
Gor. ?/?—28/8/20.**G.**
Gor. 16/9—11/11/22.**G.**
Gor. 13/9—13/12/24.**G.**
Gor. 16/1—24/4/26.**G.**
New centre cylinder.
Gor. 1/9—27/10/28.**G.**
Gor. 16/8—25/10/30.**G.**
Gor. 3/9—22/10/32.**G.**
Gor. 10/12/32—14/1/33.**L.**
Gor. 17/3—31/3/34.**H.**
Gor. 23/1—6/2/37.**G.**
Gor. 8/6—13/7/40.**G.**
Superheated boiler fitted.
Gor. 27/1—26/2/44.**G.**
Gor. 26/8—4/11/50.**C/L.**
Gor. 17/5—5/7/52.**G.**
New centre cylinder.

BOILERS:
1332.
1331 *(ex1170)* 27/3/09.
1334 *(ex1173)* 19/3/10.
1182 *(exC5 5364)* 28/6/13.
1146 *(exC4 5267)* 28/8/20.
  916 *(exC4 6085)* 13/12/24.
1707 *(exC4 6084)* 24/4/26.
1827 *(exC4 6094)* 31/3/34.
1821 *(exC4 6094)* 6/2/37.
1886 *(exO4 6311)* 13/7/40.
3247 *(exO4 6244)* 26/2/44.
3247 reno. 22112 4/11/50.

SHEDS:
Mexborough.
March 7/7/32.
Frodingham 18/12/49.
Mexborough 31/12/50.
Doncaster 10/1/54.

RENUMBERED:
6172 13/12/24.
9902 2/6/46.
69902 4/11/50.

CONDEMNED: 13/1/56.
*Into Gor. for cut up 18/2/56
but sent to Darlington for
scrapping.*

6173

Beyer, Peacock 5005.

To traffic 1/1908.

REPAIRS:
Gor. ?/?—7/8/09.**G.**
Gor. ?/?—15/11/13.**G.**
Gor. 11/12/20—12/2/21.**G.**
Gor. 7/4—22/9/23.**G.**
Gor. 7/11/25—30/1/26.**G.**
Gor. 10/3—9/6/28.**G.**
Gor. 26/7—20/9/30.**G.**
Gor. 13/8—1/10/32.**G.**
New centre cylinder.
Gor. 11/3—1/4/33.**L.**
Gor. 28/4—12/5/34.**H.**
Gor. 20/6—18/7/36.**G.**
Gor. 16/4—4/6/38.**G.**
Gor. 12/11—20/12/41.**G.**
Superheated boiler fitted.
Gor. 29/2—8/4/44.**G.**
New right hand cylinder.
Gor. 10/2—7/4/51.**G.**
Gor. 1—15/3/52.**C/L.**
Steam reversing gear repaired.
Gor. 26/7—16/8/52.**C/L.**
Steam reversing gear repaired.

BOILERS:
1334.
1332 *(ex1172)* 7/8/09.
1334 *(ex1172)* 15/11/13.
1805 *(exC4 6094)* 9/6/28.
1707 *(ex6172)* 12/5/34.
1807 *(exC4 5260)* 18/7/36.
1067 *(exO4 6225)* 20/12/41.
1886 *(ex6172)* 8/4/44.
22347 *(ex spare)* 7/4/51,
this boiler reno. from 8465.

SHEDS:
Mexborough.
March 11/7/32.
Frodingham 18/12/49.
Mexborough 10/12/50.
Immingham 15/11/53.

RENUMBERED:
1173c 22/9/23.
6173 30/1/26.
9903 2/6/46.
69903 7/4/51.

CONDEMNED: 8/3/54.
Cut up at Doncaster.

Like the Diagram 15 boiler, the two to Diag.105 had three washout plugs on the left hand shoulder of the Belpaire firebox.

On the right hand side, boilers of Diagrams 15 and 105 were identical in having two washout plugs on the shoulder of the firebox.

Only the two Diag.105 boilers were built and their special feature was not limited to the engines to which they were first fitted. As they were quite interchangeable, one was used on No.6171 (9901 later) from 7th May 1938 to 4th September 1948 and 69903 had one from 7th April 1951 to 8th March 1954 withdrawal.

Equally, both 1932 built engines changed to Diag.15, No.2798 (9904) had that type from 9th January 1937 to 25th August 1951 and 9905 from 30th March 1946 to 1st January 1957 withdrawal.

As part of his removal of Gresley influence, his successor Thompson had the booster equipment taken off those S1's so equipped. No.6171 was ex works 2nd January 1943 without it but retained the bogie to which it had changed in 1932. This had 3ft 2in. instead of 3ft 6in. wheels and its wheel base was 8ft 6in. in place of 7ft 6in. The bogie sanding was also removed.

The two which had been built with booster also had the equipment removed in 1943 but kept their outside frame bogie. No.2798 was denuded when ex works 11th December 1943 and No.2799 when out on 5th June 1943. They also lost bogie sanding.

2798

Gorton.

To traffic 28/5/32.

REPAIRS:
Gor. 22/9—27/10/34.**G.**
Gor. 21/11/36—9/1/37.**G.**
Gor. 24/6—5/8/39.**G.**
Gor. 9/3—2/5/42.**G.**
Gor. 20/11—11/12/43.**L.**
Booster removed.
Gor. 22/3—29/4/44.**L.**
Gor. 21/7—25/8/45.**G.**
Gor. 11/9—9/10/48.**G.**
Gor. 3—24/6/50.**C/H.**
Gor. 25/8—6/10/51.**G.**
Gor. 5/4—3/5/52.**C/L.**
Steam reversing gear over-hauled.
Gor. 2—16/8/52.**C/L.**

BOILERS:
8464.
1473 *(exO4 5412)* 9/1/37.
3290 *(exO4 5331)* 25/8/45.
3291 *(exO4 3823)* 9/10/48.
22348 *(ex spare)* 6/10/51,
this boiler reno. from 8464.

SHEDS:
Mexborough.*
Immingham 3/1/54.
Doncaster 14/3/54.

RENUMBERED:
9904 14/7/46.
69904 9/10/48.

CONDEMNED: 6/1/56.
Cut up at Darlington.

───────────────────

2799

Gorton.

To traffic 25/6/32.

REPAIRS:
Gor. 3/11—8/12/34.**G.**
Gor. 20/2—20/3/37.**G.**
Gor. 6/1—17/2/40.**G.**
Gor. 5/5—5/6/43.**G.**
Booster removed.
Gor. 6/4—29/4/44.**L.**
Gor. 2—30/3/46.**G.**
Gor. 8/1—5/2/49.**G.**
Gor. 21/7—18/8/51.**C/H.**
Gor. 3/4—15/5/54.**G.**

BOILERS:
8465.
8464 *(ex2798)* 20/3/37.

3326 *(exO4 6246)* 30/3/46.
3290 *(ex9904)* 5/2/49.
3290 reno.22207 18/8/51.
22220 15/5/54.

SHEDS:
Mexborough.*
Doncaster 10/1/54.
Frodingham 3/4/55.

RENUMBERED:
9905 30/3/46.
69905 5/2/49.

CONDEMNED: 1/1/57.
Into Dar. for cut up 5/1/57.

* *2799 shown in 1932 GE returns as new engine added to their stock, & GC Section return only gave 2798.*

───────────────────

Without booster the sanding to the rear coupled wheels was gravity applied with the box fillers below the running plate. The sanding to the two leading pairs of wheels had been changed to steam application before the Grouping. No further change was made to 6170, 6172 and 6173.

When the booster was put on No.6171, the rear coupled wheels sanding was changed to steam applied, the boxes were put in the cab, with the fillers through the side sheets. Steam sanding was also provided in front of the leading wheels of the bogie.

Nos.2798 and 2799 were built to the same arrangements for sanding as on No.6171 when booster fitted.

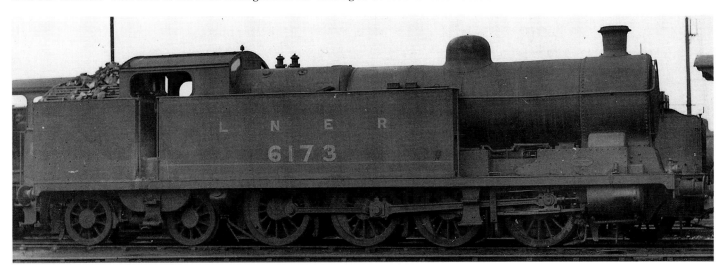

To avoid interference with track circuits when working in Whitemoor yard, rail washing equipment had been fitted when Nos.6172 (22nd) and 6173 (1st) were ex works from Gorton in October 1932.

At some time during the 1939-1945 war the rail washing gear was taken off, probably after the Thompson edict of 20th June 1941 to "Remove all gadgets". No.6173 was next ex works 20th December 1941 but No.6172 not until 26th February 1944. No.6172 was superheated from 13th July 1940 and No.6173 from 20th December 1941 but neither was then fitted with Gresley anti-vacuum valve.

By the end of 1941, five of the six were superheated but No.6170 was not dealt with until ex works 17th November 1951 by which time it was 69900. It also then got a Gresley anti-vacuum valve.

(left) Until into the 1930's the original 1ft 10in. Robinson chimney was retained but 6170, 6172 and 6173 were then changed to the 1ft 9in. plantpot type. Until January 1937 No.6172 retained Ramsbottom safety valves.

(below) Ex works 6th February 1937, No.6172, had changed to Ross 'pop' safety valves but still had the whistle on the cab roof which still gave 13ft 3½in. height from rail. Note the change of buffer head from oval to circular.

When ex works 13th July 1940, with superheater, No.6172 had also been cut to 12ft 10¹/₂in. maximum height by moving the whistle to the firebox, fitting a flatter top dome cover and a GC type chimney only 1ft 5in. tall. It was the only one so treated but No.6173 was brought below 13ft 0in. when ex works 20th December 1941 and No.6170 on 21st November 1942 by moving the whistle and fitting the same 1ft 6¹/₄in. tall built-up chimney as on the engines with booster.

No.6172 which became 9902 and 69902 kept its traditional GC type chimney through to its 13th January 1956 withdrawal, in contrast to the other five which kept the 1ft 6¹/₄in. built-up Doncaster style.

(left) Beginning with No.2798 (9904 from 14th July 1946), all had the original wheel and handle fastening for the smokebox door changed to two handles. No.9905 ex works 30th March 1946 kept the wheel and handle but had the upper lamp iron moved from the top of the smokebox on to the door *(see page 35, top)*. This move on the other five was only made after the end of the LNER.

(below) When Nos.2798 and 2799 were new, their cab footsteps were similar to those put on 6171 when it got the booster, and were open sided.

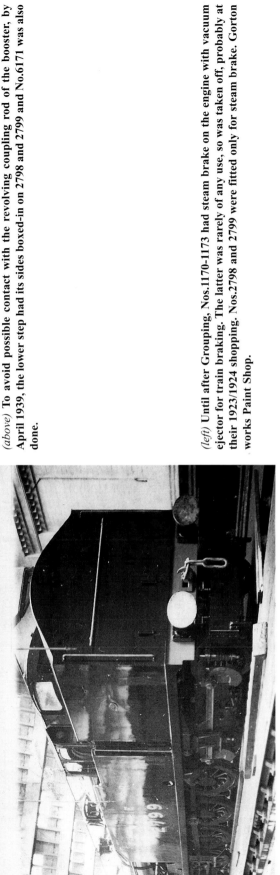

(above) To avoid possible contact with the revolving coupling rod of the booster, by April 1939, the lower step had its sides boxed-in on 2798 and 2799 and No.6171 was also done.

(left) Until after Grouping, Nos.1170-1173 had steam brake on the engine with vacuum ejector for train braking. The latter was rarely of any use, so was taken off, probably at their 1923/1924 shopping. Nos.2798 and 2799 were fitted only for steam brake. Gorton works Paint Shop.

At Grouping, the four GC engines were in black goods livery with red and white double lining and carried a transfer-applied company crest on each side tank.

To June 1928, black with single red lining was used. The first to get it would be 1173, ex works 22nd September 1923 and 1171 out 8th December 1923. It is thought that these two would carry suffix C but no photographic evidence has been found. No.6170 on 3rd May 1924 and 6172 on 13th December 1924 went straight to this style.

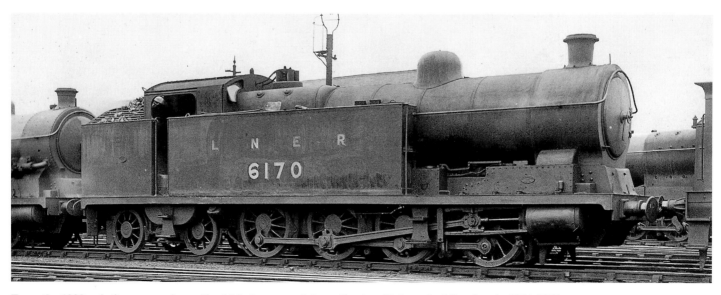

From the 1928 painting economies, unlined black was used thereafter to withdrawal of the class in 1954-1957.

Whereas 6170 to 6172 had the small maker's plate on the leading sandbox, No.6173 had been fitted with the larger plate that Beyer, Peacock had discarded about 1900. It is understood the plate was put on because No.1173 was intended for an exhibition, but it was not shown. The special plate did however survive to 8th March 1954 withdrawal. March shed.

From July 1942 only NE was used, but instead of continuing with 7½in. letters Gorton used the 12in. size. Even on so big an engine as the S1 they looked too big. No.6172 got NE from 26th February 1944 and March shed re-numbered it to 9902 on Sunday 2nd June 1946, and it stayed as shown until 26th August 1950, so it missed out on LNER and BRITISH RAILWAYS lettering.

LNER was restored from January 1946, No.6170 having it from ex works 27th April 1946. Gorton persisted with the 12in. letters, made all the more incongruous when Mexborough shed used only 6in. stencils to re-number it 9900 on Sunday 28th July 1946.

No.6171 had 7½in. LNER from its March 1941 general repair and although it was fitted with three new cylinders at a March-June 1944 repair it was not repainted and so, never had only NE. Mexborough shed used 6in. stencils to make it 9901 on Sunday 26th May 1946 and Gorton changed these to 12in. painted and unshaded figures (*see* page 34, bottom) when it was in for a light repair in September 1947.

No.6173 did not get either NE or BRITISH RAILWAYS lettering. The 7½in. LNER from its 20th December 1941 application was made to last until it went for repair on 10th February 1951. Out on 8th April 1944 from general repair it had not been re-painted and when March shed made it No.9903 on Sunday 2nd June 1946 they used 12in. shaded transfers. So it remained as shown until it went for repair on 10th February 1951. March shed.

No.2799 was the only one to get full treatment. Out on 5th June 1943 with the booster off, it had only NE but in 12in letters. From general repair, it was ex works 30th March 1946 as 9905, and with 12in. LNER all in shaded transfers from which it changed to BRITISH RAILWAYS lettering when out on 5th February 1949.

69901 and 69904 were the first to show the new ownership, both being out of Gorton on 9th October 1948 from general repair. 69900 (2nd April) and 69905 (5th February) also got this style in 1949. Note they had the correct Gill sans 6 and 9 painted on the bunker.

Starting with 69902 ex works on 4th November 1950, all six then got the small size emblem and this was their final guise.

The smokebox number plates must all have been cast at the same time as they all had the modified 6 and 9 which the paint shop had already ceased to use. Their fitting dates ranged from 9th October 1948 to as late as 4th November 1950 on 69902.

2798 new on 28th May 1932 was one of the two added to the class by the LNER. Its shed was Mexborough, as here in February 1936, for working at Wath yard. On 14th July 1946 the shed changed it to 9904 and ex works on 9th October 1948 it was 69904.

69902 from ex works 4th November 1950, had been 9902 from 2nd June 1946 and LNER 6172 from 13th December 1924. It was at Mexborough until 7th July 1932 then at March shed but on 18th December 1949 moved to Frodingham shed and on 31st December 1950 back to Mexborough. From there on 7th August 1953 it was working here at Wath and on 10th January 1954 it went to Doncaster shed from where it was withdrawn on 13th January 1956.

No.69903 was the first to be withdrawn on 8th March 1954 and by 25th April 1954 had been sent to Doncaster works to be cut-up. Note the normal 3-link loose coupling. Curiously 69905 was given a general repair from 3rd April to 15th May 1954 but this was the last works attention for the class.

In its final years 69901 changed to screw adjustable coupling, probably for its use as Doncaster shed shunter from January 1954 to April 1955.

Three S1's, 69900, 69902 and 69904 were withdrawn in January 1956 and during February arrived at Gorton only to be sent to Darlington for cutting up. 69901 and 69905 were taken out of stock on 1st January 1957 and Class S1 was then extinct. They too were cut-up in Darlington scrap yard.

Five more engines, Nos.1656 to 1660, were built at Darlington between 18th November and 15th December 1925 by the LNER. The only significant difference from the NER engines was the fitting of Ross 'pops' instead of Ramsbottom safety valves.

Until 1932 they had lever reverse but from March 1932 to August 1934 all, except 1355 and 1358, were fitted with steam reversing gear taken from K3 class engines built during 1924 and 1925. The other two had moved to the Southern area and were then on Doncaster maintenance.

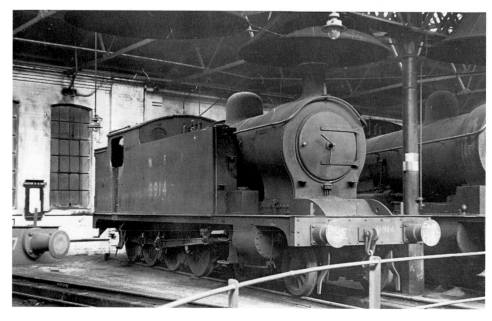

Starting with No.1350, ex works 8th March 1941, lever reverse was restored, this process being completed when 9914 (ex 1354) was ex works 3rd May 1947.

CLASS T 1

1350

Gateshead 114.

To traffic 9/1909.

REPAIRS:
???. ?/?—?/7/21.**G.**
Dar. 14/7—30/10/25.**G.**
Dar. 2/1—22/2/29.**G.**
Dar. 7—31/8/31.**L.**
Dar. 13/4—22/5/33.**G.**
Steam reverse fitted.
Dar. 8/5—19/7/35.**L.**
Dar. 30/7—14/9/37.**G.**
Back footsteps fitted.
Dar. 23/7—8/3/41.**G.**
Steam reverse removed.
Dar. 5/7—19/8/43.**G.**
Dar. 25/10—24/11/45.**G.**
Dar. 23/2—2/4/48.**G.**
Dar. 3—29/1/49.**L.**
Dar. 3/8—2/9/50.**G.**
Dar. 3/3—2/4/53.**G.**
Dar. 7—14/7/53.**N/C.**
Dar. 6/2—6/3/56.**G.**
Dar. 27—28/6/56.**N/C.**

BOILERS:
G800.
D2043 *(new)* 22/2/29.
D1636 *(ex1356)* 14/9/37.
D1982 *(ex1357)* 19/8/43.
D1786 *(ex1656)* 24/11/45.
D1793 *(ex9913)* 2/4/48.
24681 *(exA6 9795)* 2/9/50.
24704 *(ex?)* 2/4/53.
24680 *(ex69915 63B)* 6/3/56.

SHEDS:
Hull Dairycoates.
Newport 23/6/39.
York 25/9/55.
Selby 16/11/58.
York 13/9/59.

RENUMBERED:
9910 1/12/46.
69910 2/4/48.

CONDEMNED: 17/10/59.
Cut up at Darlington.

1351

Gateshead 115.

To traffic 9/1909.

REPAIRS:
Dar. 20/3—26/4/23.**L.**
Dar. 5/7—1/10/24.**G.**
Dar. 17—24/10/24.**N/C.**
Dar. 6—10/12/24.**L.**
Dar. 23/5—27/8/27.**G.**
Dar. 3/6—20/8/30.**G.**
Dar. 28/3—11/5/33.**G.**
Steam reverse fitted.
Dar. 3/1—19/2/36.**G.**
Back footsteps fitted.
Dar. 30/1—5/3/40.**G.**
Dar. 17/6—20/7/40.**L.**
After collision.
Dar. 17/3—16/4/41.**L.**
Bunker damaged.
Dar. 12/12/42—8/2/43.**G.**
Steam reverse removed.
Dar. 31/7—7/9/45.**G.**
Dar. 9/9—9/10/47.**G.**
Dar. 25/10—25/11/50.**G.**
Dar. 27—28/11/50.**N/C.**
Dar. 18/8—12/9/53.**L/I.**

BOILERS:
G801.
D1982 *(new)* 27/8/27.
D1343 *(exA6 692)* 19/2/36.
D1787 *(exA6 687)* 5/3/40.
D1793 *(ex1657)* 8/2/43.
2036 *(exA6 691)* 7/9/45.
2371 *(ex9921)* 9/10/47.
24750 *(new 63B)* 25/11/50.

SHED:
Newport.

RENUMBERED:
9911 18/8/46.
69911 25/11/50.

CONDEMNED: 19/3/57.
Cut up at Darlington.

1352

Gateshead 116.

To traffic 10/1909.

REPAIRS:
Dar. 27/5—29/9/25.**G.**
Dar. 4/7—11/9/28.**G.**
Dar. 25/6—2/9/31.**G.**
Dar. 19/4—18/5/34.**G.**
Steam reverse fitted.
Dar. 10/11—21/12/38.**G.**
Back footsteps fitted.
Dar. 7/2—25/4/39.**L.**
Dar. 24/6—30/8/41.**G.**
Dar. 4/5—2/6/44.**G.**
Steam reverse removed.
Dar. 14/4—24/5/47.**G.**
Dar. 7/11—22/12/50.**G.**
Dar. 27/5—26/6/53.**G.**
Dar. 29/12/55—25/1/56.**L/I.**

BOILERS:
G802.
D2036 *(new)* 11/9/28.
D1984 *(exA6 686)* 18/5/34.
D1354 *(ex1656)* 21/12/38.
D1791 *(exA6 686)* 2/6/44.
3617 *(new 63B)* 24/5/47.
3617 *reno.* 24692 22/12/50.
24694 *(ex69915 63B)* 26/6/53.

SHEDS:
Hull Dairycoates.
Stockton 14/9/52.
Selby 24/3/57.
York 13/9/59.

RENUMBERED:
9912 10/11/46.
69912 22/12/50.

CONDEMNED: 17/10/59.
Cut up at Darlington.

1353

Gateshead 117.

To traffic 11/1909.

REPAIRS:
???. ?/?—?/4/22.**G.**
Dar. 13/11/24—26/2/25.**G.**
Dar. 6/3—9/5/28.**G.**
Dar. 14/2—2/4/30.**G.**
Dar. 7/6—14/7/32.**G.**
Steam reverse fitted.
Dar. 21/8—17/9/34.**L.**
Dar. 31/7—10/9/36.**G.**
Back footsteps fitted.

Dar. 8/5—5/6/40.**G.**
Dar. 14/2—8/3/41.**G.**
Dar. 26/11/42—8/1/43.**G.**
Steam reverse removed.
Dar. 2—5/2/44.**N/C.**
Buffer beam painted.
Dar. 28/8—1/10/45.**G.**
Dar. 27/11/47—9/1/48.**G.**
Dar. 2/11—2/12/50.**G.**
Dar. 4—6/12/50.**N/C.**
Dar. 5—29/8/53.**H/I.**
Dar. 4/12/56. *Weigh.*
Dar. 21/11/57. *Not repaired.*

BOILERS:
G803.
G676 ?/4/22.
D1624 *(new)* 26/2/25.
2372 *(ex1657)* 5/6/40.
D1793 *(ex1351)* 1/10/45.
2036 *(ex9911)* 9/1/48.
24751 *(new 63B)* 2/12/50.

SHEDS:
Newport.
York 28/10/56.

RENUMBERED:
9913 18/8/46.
69913 2/12/50.

CONDEMNED: 16/12/57.
Cut up at Darlington.

1354

Gateshead 118.

To traffic 12/1909.

REPAIRS:
???. ?/?—?/10/20.**G.**
Dar. 11/10—5/12/24.**L.**
Dar. 21/9—31/12/25.**G.**
Dar. 20/12/28—15/2/29.**G.**
Dar. 1/2—16/3/32.**G.**
Steam reverse fitted.
Dar. 25/1—24/2/38.**G.**
Back footsteps fitted.
Dar. 25/2—2/3/38.**N/C.**
Dar. 25/2—17/4/41.**G.**
Dar. 30/11—24/12/42.**L.**
Dar. 15/8—29/9/44.**G.**
Superheated boiler fitted.
Dar. 14/3—3/5/47.**G.**
Steam reverse removed.

WORKS CODES:- Bpk - Beyer, Peacock. Cow - Cowlairs. Dar- Darlington. Don - Doncaster. Ghd - Gateshead. Gor - Gorton. Inv - Inverurie. Str - Stratford. Wrx - Wrexham.
REPAIR CODES:- **C/H** - Casual Heavy. **C/L** - Casual Light. **G** - General. **H** - Heavy. **H/I** - Heavy Intermediate. **L** - Light. **L/I** - Light Intermediate. **N/C** - Non-Classified.

51

Only one T1 was ever superheated, No.1354 ex works 29th September 1944 which had been fitted with a newly built Diagram 63B boiler. This type could be identified by the position of the dome, 1ft 9in. further back, and the square shape of the cover. Note the buffer beams were painted white to aid visibility during ARP blackout conditions.

Although a boiler change was made at 69914's August 1949 repair, it was to another 63B superheated type boiler. 69914 next went to works on 4th December 1951 and when ex works 29th December it had reverted to a non-superheated type.

The original boiler on all fifteen was to Diagram 61 and all replacements and spares until 1935 were to that Diagram. One built in June 1930 started work on No.1658 in October 1933, passed to 1659 in July 1940 and then on to 9911 in October 1947 until October 1950. It then served 69916 from 17th February 1951 to 12th August 1957 when both engine and boiler were withdrawn. It was the last Diagram 61 boiler and 69916 (ex1357) was the only T1 to use only Diagram 61 boilers all through its life, except for the early withdrawals 1355 and 1358.

In 1935 five superheated boilers were built to Diagram 63C and were used almost entirely on 4-6-2T engines. In December 1949 one had its superheater taken out and was then used on 69922 from 14th December 1949 to 25th June 1952 and by 69919 from 6th September 1952 to 21st February 1955 when boiler and engine were both withdrawn.

Another boiler variation occurred with 69917 from July 1955. After starting work in May 1935 a Diagram 63A boiler served on six A8 class engines until January 1954. The superheater was then taken out and this boiler was used on 69917 from 16th July 1955 until 2nd November 1959 when boiler and engine were withdrawn.

In 1945, replacements were needed for the boilers built for the 1925 batch of engines so Darlington built five to diagram 63B but without the superheater and these were used entirely on T1 class starting with No.1657 in October 1945 and 1359 in June 1946. Four more were built and put to work on T1 class between November 1950 and February 1952 plus one 63B built in 1939 and from which the superheater was removed in October 1949. Diagram 63B had the dome 1ft 9in. further back than the others and had a squarer shaped cover to it.

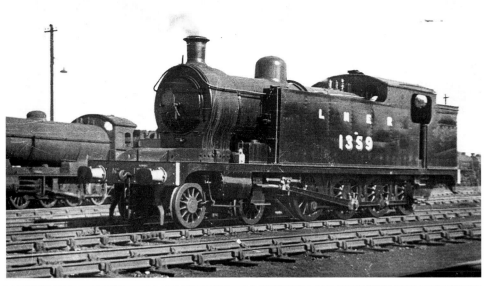

(above) Although the boilers built with the five 1925 engines had 'pop' valves, they were on a raised mounting, but starting with five boilers built in November 1927, as replacements for the 1909/1910 batch, the 'pop' valves were put directly on to the firebox. Because the same base casing was used, this gave the impression that shorter valves were being used.

(right) Diagram 61 boilers could be easily recognised as the blower control rod was very prominent on the left-hand side. On all other boiler types used on T1 class, this control rod was internal. 69910 was the last one noted to be carrying the cover around the base of the safety valves.

1354 cont./
Dar. 23/6—10/8/49.**G.**
Dar. 4—29/12/51.**G.**
Saturated boiler fitted.
Dar. 1—4/1/52.**N/C.**
Dar. 3/8/55. *Not repaired.*

BOILERS:
  G804.
  G658 ?/10/20.
  D1629 *(new)* 31/12/25.
  D1630 *(exA6 691)* 24/2/38.
    3364 *(new, sup.63B)* 29/9/44.
    3361 *(exA8 9865 63B)* 10/8/49.
    24754 *(new, sat.63B)* 29/12/51.

SHEDS:
Selby.
Newport 28/7/46.
Selby 8/9/46.
Hull Dairycoates 6/2/49.
Tyne Dock 14/9/52.
Stockton 13/3/55.

RENUMBERED:
  9914 3/11/46.
  69914 10/8/49.

CONDEMNED: 15/8/55.
Cut up at Darlington.

1355

Gateshead 119.

To traffic 12/1909.

REPAIRS:
???. ?/?—14/7/22.**?.**
Ghd. 3/3—11/5/25.**G.**
Dar. 11/3—8/4/27.**L.**
Ghd. 19/11—15/1/29.**G.**
Ghd. 4/8—8/9/31.**G.**
Gor. ?/?—13/5/33.**L.**
Rail washing gear fitted.
Don.. 22/5—6/7/34.**G.**
New wood buffer beams fitted.

BOILERS:
  G807.
D2042 *(new)* 15/1/29.

SHEDS:
Tyne Dock.
March 7/6/32.
Doncaster 26/4/34.
Mexborough 1/8/34.
King's Cross 16/6/36.
Doncaster 9/8/36.

CONDEMNED: 8/5/37.
Cut up at Doncaster.

1356

Gateshead 120.

To traffic 2/1910.

REPAIRS:
Dar. 14/5—9/8/23.**G.**
Dar. 28/8—30/8/23.**N/C.**
Dar. 21/3—30/7/27.**G.**
Ghd. 22/12/27—24/1/28.**L.**
Ghd. 14/2—1/3/28.**L.**
Dar. 17—21/9/28.**L.**
Dar. 26/10—9/11/28.**N/C.**
Dar. 14/5—11/6/30.**N/C.**
Dar. 22/9—14/10/30.**N/C.**
Dar. 17/12/30—22/1/31.**N/C.**
Dar. 29/5—18/6/31.**N/C.**
Ghd. 22/3—27/4/32.**G.**
Steam reverse fitted.
Dar. 18/1—20/2/37.**G.**
Back footsteps fitted.
Dar. 15/7—6/11/40.**G.**
Dar. 6/3—1/4/44.**G.**
Steam reverse removed.
Dar. 13/3—26/4/47.**G.**
Dar. 6/7—14/10/49.**G.**
Dar. 11—19/12/50.**C/L.**
Dar. 28/6—17/7/51.**G.**
Radio equipment fitted.
Dar. 22/1—20/2/53.**G.**
Dar. 17/1—9/2/56.**G.**
Dar. 8/4/57—15/5/58.**C/L.**
Dar. 10/3/59. *Not repaired.*

BOILERS:
  G808.
  D1636 *(new)* 30/7/27.
  D1790 *(ex1659)* 20/2/37.
  D1343 *(exA6 694)* 1/4/44.
  D1625 *(ex9922)* 26/4/47.
    3065 *(exA8 9853 63B)*
      14/10/49.
    3065 reno.24694 19/12/50.
  24680 *(ex69919 63B)* 20/2/53.
  24722 *(ex69917 63B)* 9/2/56.

SHEDS:
Tyne Dock.
Hull Dairycoates 15/4/35.
Newport 15/7/51.
York 25/9/55.
Selby 8/7/56.

RENUMBERED:
  9915 7/7/46.
  69915 14/10/49.

CONDEMNED: 16/3/59.
Cut up at Darlington.

1357

Gateshead 121.

To traffic 3/1910.

REPAIRS:
???. ?/?—?/1/22.**?.**
Ghd. 20/8—11/9/23.**L.**
Ghd. 29/6—7/10/25.**G.**
Ghd. 14/2—8/3/28.**L.**
Dar. 5/10—27/11/28.**G.**
Dar. 13—26/5/30.**N/C.**
Dar. 19—30/1/31.**N/C.**
Dar. 18—29/5/31.**N/C.**
Dar. 24/2—3/3/32.**N/C.**
Ghd. 12/7—18/8/32.**G.**
Steam reverse fitted.
Dar. 27/1—4/4/36.**G.**
Back footsteps fitted.
Dar. 6/6/36.**N/C.**
Dar. 25/5—8/7/39.**G.**
Dar. 18—20/7/39.**N/C.**
Dar. 24/7—6/9/39.**N/C.**
Dar. 18/12/39—2/1/40.**N/C.**
Dar. 6/2—4/4/40.**H.**
Dar. 14/5—21/6/43.**G.**
Dar. 22/11—29/12/45.**G.**
Steam reverse removed.
Dar. 4/3—13/4/48.**G.**
Dar. 24/1—17/2/51.**G.**
Dar. 5—7/3/51.**N/C.**
Dar. 9—16/8/51.**C/L.**
Dar. 24/9—17/10/53.**H/I.**
Dar. 19—20/10/53.**N/C.**
Dar. 4—7/11/53.**N/C.**
Dar. 25—30/11/53.**N/C.**
Dar. 8/8/57.*Not repaired.*

BOILERS:
  G817.
  2037 *(new)* 27/11/28.
  D1982 *(ex1351)* 4/4/36.
  D1984 *(ex1660)* 21/6/43.
  D1982 *(ex1350)* 29/12/45.
  2037 *(exA6 9795)* 13/4/48.
  24701 *(ex9911)* 17/2/51.

SHEDS:
Tyne Dock.
Newport 29/6/42.
York 25/9/55.

RENUMBERED:
  9916 10/11/46.
  69916 13/4/48.

CONDEMNED: 12/8/57.
Cut up at Darlington.

1358

Gateshead 122.

To traffic 4/1910.

REPAIRS:
Ghd. 29/8—31/10/23.**G.**
Ghd. 4/11—6/12/24.**L.**
Ghd. 3/11/27—19/1/28.**G.**
Str. ?/?—?/10/30.**G.**
Gor. 25/2—18/3/33.**L.**
Rail washing gear fitted.
Don. 23/4—12/6/36.**G.**

BOILERS:
  G818.
  D2039 *(new)* 19/1/28.

SHEDS:
Tyne Dock.
Selby 20/1/28.
March 14/1/29.
Doncaster 10/4/34.
Mexborough 2/5/34.
Doncaster 30/5/34.

RENUMBERED:
1358D 31/10/23 to 4/11/24.

CONDEMNED: 8/5/37.
Cut up at Doncaster.

1359

Gateshead 123.

To traffic 4/1910.

REPAIRS:
Ghd. 18/9—26/11/23.**G.**
Ghd. 16/4—28/7/26.**G.**
Dar. 17/6—27/8/31.**G.**
Dar. 3/5—11/6/34.**G.**
Steam reverse fitted.
Dar. 12/8—23/9/37.**G.**
Back footsteps fitted.
Dar. 27/8—26/3/41.**G.**
Dar. 24/3—3/4/43.**N/C.**
Dar. 30/11—9/12/43.**L.**
Dar. 24/7—20/9/44.**G.**
Dar. 25/4—1/6/46.**G.**
Steam reverse removed.
Dar. 27/8—3/9/46.**N/C.**
Alteration to Downs' sanding.
Dar. 17/4—26/5/48.**G.**
Dar. 10/9—6/10/51.**G.**
Dar. 19/9/53—13/1/54.**C/H.**
Dar. 17/6—16/7/55.**G.**
Dar. 18—21/7/55.**N/C.**

BOILERS:
G826.

The normal chimney was 1ft 11⁷/₈in. tall giving a height from rail of 13ft 1in. and none ever carried a windjabber.

From August 1947 No.9921, and from 9th January 1948 No.9913, each carried a 3¹/₂in. shorter chimney, spare from A7 class, purely for expediency and availability. From 29th August 1953 No.69913 regained a chimney of normal height, as did 69921 by December 1955.

Until 1932 there were no lifting holes in the front end of the frames and they were not put in until the lifting facilities at Darlington works were changed in that year.

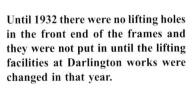

All fifteen duly had lifting holes put in, 1355 and 1358 also getting them although no longer on Darlington maintenance.

Both NER and LNER built batches had wheel and handle fastening for the smokebox door until into the 1930's.

Between about 1933 and 1935 the thirteen in NE Area had the wheel replaced by a second handle, but 1355 and 1358 still had a wheel when they were withdrawn on 8th May 1937.

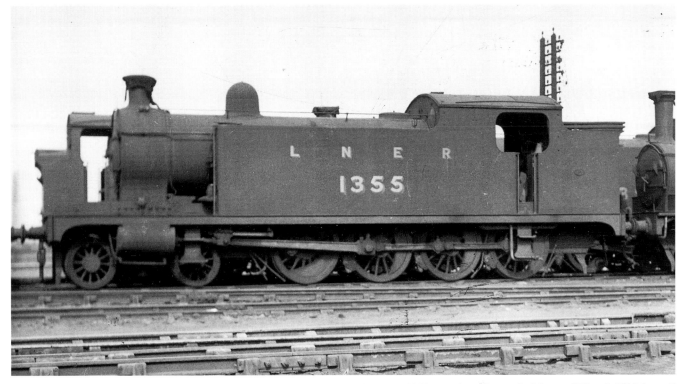

In connection with their work on hump shunting in Whitemoor yard, 1355 and 1358 went into Gorton in May and March 1933 for rail washing gear to be fitted. This was for removal of sand which might interfere with track circuits.

Whilst they still had lever reverse, the front end of the side tanks were joined by an equalising pipe just above the top edge of the frame plates.

To enable steam-reversing gear to be fitted, it was necessary to remove the equalising pipe, leaving the levelling to be done through the tank in the bunker.

Removal of the equalising pipe, and then the 1941-1947 change back to lever reverse enabled much larger sand boxes to be fitted, starting with No.1359 in June 1946 (*see* page 55, top). By the end of 1947, six Nos.1359 (9917) and 9912, 9914, 9915, 9920 and 9922 had the larger boxes which also had the Downs' heating coil in them to keep the sand dry.

1359 cont./
D1630 *(new)* 28/7/26.
D2036 *(ex1352)* 11/6/34.
D2043 *(ex1350)* 23/9/37.
  3618 *(new 63B)* 1/6/46.
  3618 *reno.24722* 6/10/51.
24698 *(exA8 69873, saturated 63A)* 16/7/55.

SHEDS:
Tyne Dock.
Gateshead ?/12/24.
Selby 16/1/29.
Newport 22/9/44.
Consett 10/6/56.
Tyne Dock 15/2/59.

RENUMBERED:
  1359ᴅ 26/11/23 to 16/4/26.
  9917 17/11/46.
  69917 26/5/48.

CONDEMNED: 2/11/59.
Cut up at Darlington.

_____

1656

Darlington.

To traffic 18/11/25.

REPAIRS:
Dar. 8/10—27/11/28.**G.**
Ghd. 21/9—1/12/32.**H.**
Dar. 22/6—2/8/34.**G.**
Steam reverse fitted.
Dar. 4/4—26/5/38.**G.**
Back footsteps fitted.
Dar. 22/12/41—21/3/42.**G.**
Dar. 22/3—25/4/44.**G.**
Dar. 6/9—6/10/45.**G.**
Steam reverse removed.
Dar. 17/9—17/10/47.**G.**
Dar. 25/11/49—11/1/50.**G.**
Dar. 14/1—9/2/52.**G.**
Dar. 12/1—4/2/54.**H/I.**
Dar. 8—10/2/54.**N/C.**
Dar. 1/10/58.*Not repaired.*

BOILERS:
D1786.
D1354 *(exA6 691)* 2/8/34.
D1629 *(ex1354)* 26/5/38.
D1786 *(exA6 688)* 21/3/42.
  2372 *(ex1353)* 6/10/45.
  3620 *(ex9919 63B)* 17/10/47.
24759 *(new, 63B)* 9/2/52.

SHEDS:
York.
Selby 30/11/25.
York 8/1/26.
March 18/1/29.
Tyne Dock 7/6/32.
Newport 28/3/43.
Stockton 30/3/43.
Hull Dairycoates 16/6/57.
Goole 28/7/57.

RENUMBERED:
  9918 3/11/46.
  69918 11/1/50.

CONDEMNED: 1/10/58.
Cut up at Darlington.

_____

1657

Darlington.

To traffic 21/11/25.

REPAIRS:
Dar. 16/7—12/9/29.**G.**
Dar. 18/4—26/5/32.**G.**
Steam reverse fitted.
Dar. 27/12/34—14/2/35.**G.**
Dar. 23/4—22/5/40.**G.**
Back footsteps fitted.
Dar. 8—17/7/42.**N/C.**
Dar. 30/12/42—1/2/43.**G.**
Dar. 3/9—3/10/45.**G.**
Steam reverse removed.
Dar. 4/7—23/8/47.**G.**
Dar. 11/7—26/8/50.**G.**
Dar. 28—30/8/50.**N/C.**
Dar. 13/8—6/9/52.**G.**
Dar. 8—9/9/52.**N/C.**
Dar. 17—24/6/54.**C/L.**
Dar. 26/1/55. *Not repaired.*

BOILERS:
D1787.
  2372 *(new)* 14/2/35.
D1793 *(exA6 694)* 22/5/40.
D1787 *(ex1351)* 1/2/43.
  3620 *(new, 63B)* 3/10/45.
  3613 *(new, 63B)* 23/8/47.
  3613 *reno.24680* 26/8/50.
24725 *(ex69922, sat.63C)* 6/9/52.

SHEDS:
Stockton 20/11/25.
Bullcroft 9/7/30.
York 19/7/30.
Hull Dairycoates 17/12/30.
Blaydon 24/6/42.

Newport 28/3/43.
Hull Dairycoates 15/7/51.
Stockton 14/9/52.

RENUMBERED:
  9919 18/8/46.
  69919 26/8/50.

CONDEMNED: 21/2/55.
Cut up at Darlington.

_____

1658

Darlington.

To traffic 26/11/25.

REPAIRS:
Dar. 13/5—4/7/29.**G.**
Dar. 1/9—18/10/33.**G.**
Steam reverse fitted.
Dar. 17/3—23/4/37.**G.**
Back footsteps fitted.
Dar. 1—25/6/40.**G.**
Dar. 22/6—30/8/43.**G.**
Steam reverse removed.
Dar. 6—15/10/43.**L.**
Dar. 29/3—16/5/47.**G.**
Dar. 30/10—2/12/50.**G.**
Dar. 8/10—6/11/54.**G.**
Dar. 11/11/54—6/1/55.**N/C.**
Dar. 9/1/59.*Not repaired.*

BOILERS:
D1790.
  2371 *(new)* 18/10/33.
D1624 *(ex1353)* 25/6/40.
D1636 *(ex1350)* 30/8/43.
  3614 *(new, 63B)* 16/5/47.
  3614 *reno.24691* 2/12/50.

SHEDS:
Stockton.
York 9/7/30.
Bullcroft 19/7/30.
Hull Dairycoates 12/10/31.
Tyne Dock 26/11/50.

RENUMBERED:
  9920 15/12/46.
  69920 2/12/50.

CONDEMNED: 12/1/59.
Cut up at Darlington.

_____

1659

Darlington.

To traffic 4/12/25.

REPAIRS:
Dar. 14/2—9/4/29.**G.**
Dar. 31/10—3/12/29.**L.**
Dar. 31/8—13/10/31.**G.**
Dar. 4/1—2/2/34.**G.**
Steam reverse fitted.
Dar. 15/10—28/11/36.**G.**
Back footsteps fitted.
Dar. 11/6—3/7/40.**G.**
Dar. 15/2—30/4/43.**G.**
Dar. 16/2—13/3/44.**L.**
Dar. 3/7—18/8/45.**G.**
Steam reverse removed.
Dar. 12/7—23/8/47.**G.**
Dar. 29/12/50—27/1/51.**G.**
Dar. 29—30/1/51.**N/C.**
Dar. 22/6—17/7/53.**G.**
Dar. 21/11—15/12/55.**G.**
Dar. 12/6/61. *Not repaired.*

BOILERS:
D1791.
D1790 *(ex1658)* 2/2/34.
  2037 *(ex1357)* 28/11/36.
  2371 *(ex1658)* 3/7/40.
D1989 *(exA6 690)* 23/8/47.
24696 *(ex9913)* 27/1/51.
24692 *(ex69912 63B)* 17/7/53.
24754 *(ex69914 63B)* 15/12/55.

SHEDS:
Haverton Hill.
Newport 8/2/26.
Stockton 4/9/55.
Hull Dairycoates 16/6/57.
Goole 28/7/57.
Selby 25/1/59.
Tyne Dock 13/9/59.

RENUMBERED:
  9921 12/10/46.
  69921 27/1/51.

CONDEMNED: 12/6/61.
Cut up at Darlington.

_____

1660

Darlington.

To traffic 15/12/25.

REPAIRS:
Dar. 23/4—21/6/29.**G.**

WORKS CODES:- Bpk - Beyer, Peacock. Cow - Cowlairs. Dar- Darlington. . Don - Doncaster. Ghd - Gateshead. Gor - Gorton. Inv - Inverurie. Str - Stratford. Wrx - Wrexham.
REPAIR CODES:- **C/H** - Casual Heavy. **C/L** - Casual Light. **G** - General. **H**- Heavy. **H/I** - Heavy Intermediate. **L** - Light. **L/I** - Light Intermediate. **N/C** - Non-Classified.

61

Although 69919 (as 1657) had steam reversing gear taken off in October 1945, it did not get the large sandboxes until ex works 6th September 1952 but the thirteen survivors all get them (*see* page 54, middle, showing 69919 so fitted).

Starting with No.1656 in April 1944, alterations to the fixing of the side tanks were made. This involved fitting an inverted T-section arch ring to join the tops of the tanks for mutual support. All thirteen were dealt with by May 1947. Note the extra coal rail on the side and three rails across the back.; 1352 was the only engine so fitted.

Until August 1945 the smokebox door was the usual NER design with flat flange, flush fitting on the front plate. Note the protection plate above the cab opening.

The more dished design with a pressed joint ring was introduced to T1 class in August 1945 when No.1659 was so fitted and all thirteen had it by 6th October 1951. 69917 (*see* page 74, top) was the last to have a NER design door.

Ex works 17th July 1951, 69915 had been fitted for trial of a radio link between the control tower and the engine when working on the hump at Newport yard. Note the aerial above the cab roof and the battery box below the bunker. The date of removal was not recorded. Note the appropriately waggish graffiti.

1660 cont./
Dar. 4/8—15/9/32.**G**.
Steam reverse fitted.
Dar. 3/6—1/8/35.**G**.
Dar. 12/5—23/6/39.**G**.
Back footsteps fitted.
Dar. 1/5—9/6/43.**G**.
Steam reverse removed.
Dar. 14/10—16/11/46.**G**.
Dar. 26/10—14/12/49.**G**.
Dar. 20/12/50—20/1/51.**C/L**.
Dar. 25/6—18/7/52.**G**.
Ghd. 27/10—24/11/54.**C/H**.
Dar. 16/10/56. *Not repaired.*

BOILERS:
D1793.
D1625 *(exA6 687)* 1/8/35.
D1984 *(ex1352)* 23/6/39.
D1625 *(exA6 687)* 9/6/43.
  2043 *(ex1359)* 16/11/46.
  2823 *(exA6 9791, saturated
      63C)* 14/12/49.
24718 *(ex69918, 63B)* 18/7/52.

SHEDS:
Haverton Hill.
Hull Dairycoates 24/2/26.
Bullcroft 8/12/30.
Hull Dairycoates 12/10/31.
Newport 14/9/52.
York 25/9/55.

RENUMBERED:
 9922 7/7/46.
69922 14/12/49.

CONDEMNED: 22/10/56.
Cut up at Darlington.

The use of the radio equipment was not long lasting and it was probably removed at the 22nd January - 20th February 1953 general repair.

The first ten engines had twin whistles above the cab roof, one large and one small bell shape.

The five LNER built engines, 1656 to 1660 (*see* page 50, top) also had twin whistles but they were in front of the cab and the larger bell shape had been superseded by an organ pipe. When the 1927, and later built boilers were put on 1350 to 1359 they too changed to this whistle arrangement.

The Diagram 63B boilers had a single bell-shape whistle above an isolating valve mounted directly on to the firebox.

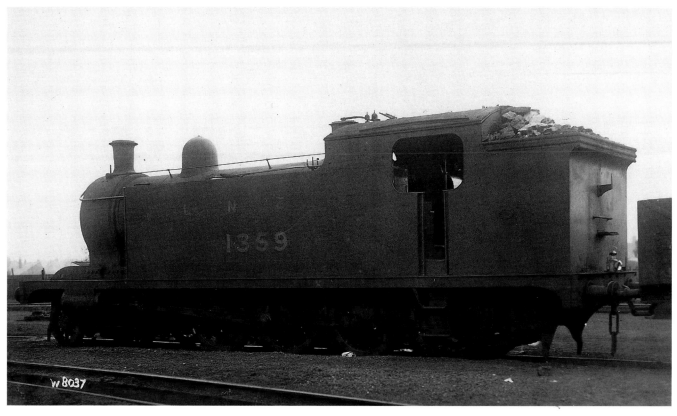

For rear access to the coal bunker its back plate was fitted with a short handgrip and a single step which was extremely difficult to use, but it was 1936 before improvement was effected.

Beginning with No.1351, ex works 19th February 1936, a footstep was fitted under each end of the rear buffer beam with a vertical handrail almost the full height of the bunker. This fitting was completed when 1657 was ex works 22nd May 1940 but 1355 and 1358 did not survive to have it applied to them.

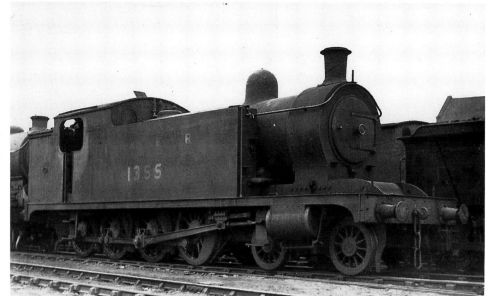

The NER engines had taper shank buffers with an end collar, solid spindle and circular head. Their flange was also circular.

Similar buffers were also provided for 1656 to 1660 except the heads were elliptical. This style was then used on 1350 to 1359 when replacement was made.

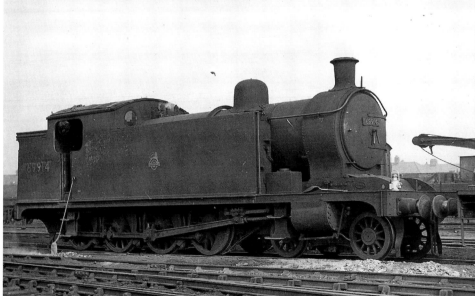

The first to acquire Group Standard buffer and draw gear was No. 1354 (9914 later), ex works 24th February 1938. These had stepped shank with a hollow spindle and square flange, the head being circular and of larger diameter. Nos.1353 and 1657 got them in 1940 and 69911, 69916, 69917, 69918 and 69921 also got them at unrecorded dates.

(above) In July 1951, 69915 was fitted with Group Standard draw hook but kept the original pattern buffers. Because the draw hook was longer, it was necessary to put circular wood packing between flange and the sandwich buffer beam.

(below) 69920 was another to have these circular packings because it also got GS draw hook. Note the change to original design buffers with small circular head, although as No.1658 it had elliptical when it was new, as in the following illustration.

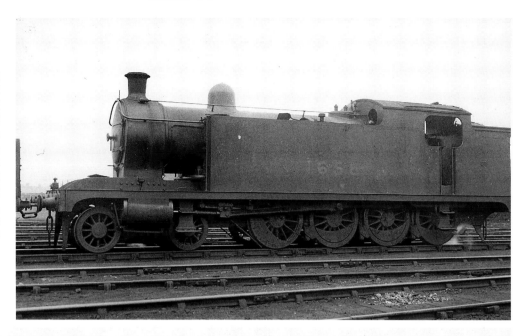

Lubrication for cylinders and valves was by double sight feed in the cab and the pipes could be seen between the front end of the tanks and rear of the smokebox. The only change was to No.1354 which, when superheated, got a mechanical lubricator on the left hand running plate, (*see* page 52), which it then retained when the superheater was taken off (*see* page 53).

(*above*) The only brake carried by the whole class was steam with no provision for train braking. The leading pair of coupled wheels did not have brake gear.

To ease access to the upper lamp iron above the smokebox, the NER added a step to the front of the smokebox waist on the right hand side.

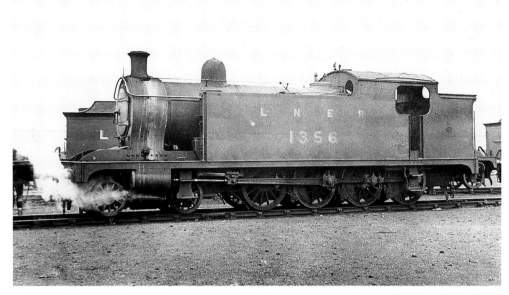

When 1656 to 1660 were new, not only were they fitted with a step on the right hand side, but they had a similar one on the left hand side. This second step was then added to all except 1358 of the original ten T1's (*see* page 58, top).

(above) The NER engines had black paint with thin red lining and at least to 1917 carried Armorial and the 24in. wide brass number plate.

(left) Only three had 1923 repaints, none having any of the variation from LNER. No.1356 (9th August) was followed by 1358D (31st October) and 1359D (26th November) all done at Gateshead works. Note Class X on the buffer beam which was still used to 1932 before the change to T1 was made.

From June 1928 through to withdrawal only unlined black was used.

Until July 1942 ownership continued to be shown as LNER in 7½in. shaded transfers. Nos.1355 and 1358 were in that guise when withdrawn in May 1937. Starting with No.1353, ex works 8th January 1943, only NE was put on, but 12in. shaded transfers were used for it. All thirteen survivors got that style, No.1657 from 1st February 1943.

From January 1946, LNER was restored but only No.1359 got it whilst in the original numbering, and this was the last T1 to be done with shaded transfers.

In the 1946 renumbering, numbers 9910 to 9922 were given to T1 class Nos.1350 to 1354, 1356, 1357, 1359 and 1656 to 1660, but No.1350 (9910) never had LNER again.

Between 16th November 1946 (9922) and 9th January 1948 (9913), 9911 to 9916 and 9918 to 9922 acquired this style of yellow painted and unshaded Gill sans but with Doncaster's modification to figures 6 and 9.

No.1350 was ex works 24th November 1945 with 12in. NE, and on Sunday 1st December 1946 Newport shed made it 9910 in the style of 9921 above. As such it went to works on 23rd February 1948 and was out on 2nd April as 69910 BRITISH RAILWAYS. Note the number moved from tank to bunker.

No.69916, ex works 13th April 1948 and 69917 out 26th May 1948, were in the same style as 69910 and these three only had the BR number put on the buffer beam. Note 12in. figures on the bunker including modified 6 and 9. No more got **BRITISH RAILWAYS** lettering until 69914 was ex works 10th August 1949 which was also the only other to do so. By then, bunker figures were 10in. to match the letters and 6 and 9 were true Gill sans both on the bunker and on the smokebox numberplate.

The other nine, 69911, 69912, 69913, 69915, and 69918 to 69922 went direct from LNER to the 15½in. size BR emblem between 14th October 1949 (69915) and 27th January 1951 (69921). The four with lettering also got this style as follows:- 69910 (2nd September 1950), 69914 (29th December 1951), 69916 (17th February 1951) and 69917 (6th October 1951). All thirteen were in this guise when they were withdrawn, no repainting being done after 69910 was out on 6th March 1956.

BR withdrawals began with 69919 on 21st February 1955 and from 2nd November 1959 only one remained, but 69921 kept on working (as here on 25th August 1960) until 12th June 1961 when its withdrawal made Class T1 extinct.

No.1350, new in September 1909, was designed for marshalling loaded coal wagons at Tyne Dock, Newport, Gascoigne Wood and Hull Dairycoates. Even before it was finish painted, its power was tested by hauling this 1000-ton train from Morpeth to Newcastle. It had LNER put on 30th October 1925 and it worked at Hull Dairycoates until 23rd June 1939 when it moved to Newport. On 1st December 1946 they changed it to 9910 and ex works 2nd April 1948 it was 69910. On 25th September 1955 it went to York, moved to Selby on 16th November 1958 and on 13th September 1959 back to York from where it was withdrawn on 17th October 1959.

No.1352, new in October 1909, was used for the official photo of the class and it too worked at Hull Dairycoates, having LNER from 29th September 1925 and being changed to 9912 on 10th November 1946. Ex works 22nd December 1950 it was 69912 and on 14th September 1952 moved to Stockton, then on 24th March 1957 to Selby and on 13th September 1959 to York, to be withdrawn on 17th October 1959.

69918 from 11th January 1950, continued working at Stockton until 16th June 1957 and then moved to Hull Dairycoates and on 28th July 1957 they sent it to the former Lancashire & Yorkshire Railway shed at Goole where it is working on the lines in the docks. Although on strange ground, it was doing the job for which the class had been designed 50 years before, the movement of coal to the side of ships for export. It was withdrawn on 1st October 1958.

WREXHAM, MOLD & CONNAH'S QUAY 400B

400B

Built 1846.
Rebuilt 1858.
Rebuilt 1880 as 0-8-0ST
Rebuilt 1888 as 0-6-2ST.
Rebuilt 1892 as 0-6-2ST.
Rebuilt 1903 as 0-8-0ST.

REPAIRS:
Gor. 1/5—12/6/15.**G**.

BOILER:
1157.

SHED:
Wrexham.

CONDEMNED: 3/8/23.
Cut up at Gorton.

This 0-6-2T was the origin of the only 0-8-0T which came into the LNER at 1st January 1923. Numbered 6 in Wrexham, Mold & Connah's Quay stock, the engine was effectively the product of a substantial rebuilding at Wrexham works in 1892 when new frames and a new saddle tank were combined with parts of an older locomotive. Another rebuilding in 1903 changed it to an 0-8-0T and a new boiler was put on.

On 1st January 1905, the Great Central Railway absorbed the WM&CQ and changed No.6 to 400B. On 1st January 1923 they passed it on to the LNER who withdrew the engine on 3rd August of the same year, before they had settled their classification system, so GCR 400B did not get either LNER class or number.